"If you look in the mirror an[...] [...]s are you need to adjust your [...] p you see yourself through God's eyes and motivate you to reflect his light to others."

—**Craig Groeschel**, senior pastor, LifeChurch.tv; author, *Soul Detox, Clean Living in a Contaminated World*

"In this helpful book, Pastor Miles shows us that unless we see ourselves biblically we will have a false identity that leads to a life of misery."

—**Mark Driscoll**, founding and preaching pastor, Mars Hill Church; *NY Times* bestselling author

"*In God in the Mirror*, Miles McPherson provides the cure to spiritual and identity myopia by applying the corrective lens embedded in the *imago Dei*, the image of God. Miles leads us in a journey of purpose, passion, and promise as we activate the image of God in us so we can engage in the habits of Christ with those around us."

—**Rev. Samuel Rodriguez**, president, National Hispanic Christian Leadership Conference, Hispanic Evangelical Association

"When Socrates said that 'the unexamined life is not worth living,' he gave a principle but did not offer a standard for conducting the examination. Miles McPherson gives us the standard—the Most High God—as well as principles flowing from the astounding truth that we are made in the image of God. *God in the Mirror* may be the most transformative volume you will read this year."

—**Frank Wright, PhD**, president and CEO, National Religious Broadcasters (NRB)

"Miles McPherson's unique take on 'made in the image of God' delivers on the promise found in the book's title. No one who reads this will ever look in the mirror and see themselves the same way again."

—**Dr. Tony Evans**, senior pastor, Oak Cliff Bible Fellowship; president, The Urban Alternative

GOD IN THE MIRROR

Discovering Who You Were Created to Be

MILES MCPHERSON

BakerBooks

a division of Baker Publishing Group
Grand Rapids, Michigan

© 2013 by Miles McPherson

Published by Baker Books
a division of Baker Publishing Group
P.O. Box 6287, Grand Rapids, MI 49516-6287
www.bakerbooks.com

Printed in the United States of America

Library of Congress Cataloging-in-Publication Data
McPherson, Miles.
    God in the mirror : discovering who you were created to be / Miles McPherson.
        p.   cm.
    Includes bibliographical references.
    ISBN 978-0-8010-1333-1 (cloth)
    1. Identity (Psychology)—Religious aspects—Christianity. 2. Self-perception—Religious aspects—Christianity. 3. Christian life. I. Title.
BV4509.5.M3675   2013
248.4—dc23   2012044720

To protect the privacy of those whose stories have been shared by the author, some names and details have been changed.

The internet addresses, email addresses, and phone numbers in this book are accurate at the time of publication. They are provided as a resource. Baker Publishing Group does not endorse them or vouch for their content or permanence.

The author is represented by the literary agency of Alive Communications, Inc., 7680 Goddard Street, Suite 200, Colorado Springs, Colorado 80920, www.alivecommunications.com

13   14   15   16   17   18   19   7   6   5   4   3   2

Contents

Are You Ready for This?

I am amazing.

Yes, you read that right.

I'm completely amazing, and I can prove it.

Now that I have your attention, let me say something about you: You are more amazing and wonderful than you know.

This book is about the *real* you, about the you God created you to be. But who is that person and how is that person supposed to live?

Charles and Khristi Cunningham, a biracial couple from Akron, Ohio, gave birth to a set of twins in 2010. Having twins is not necessarily odd in itself, but having biracial twins is a one-in-a-million occurrence. One of the children, Triniti, is white with blonde hair and blue eyes, and the other, Gabe, came out with African-American brown skin and facial features. Because they look so different from each other, some people question whether they are brother and sister.

This leads me to the big question: Since we were created in God's image for the purpose of living as His children, what does God expect to see when He looks at *us*?

Our society is in the midst of an image crisis. In our thirst for significance and a unique identity, we chase money, power, success, or fame. We pour ourselves into dead-end relationships hoping to find validation. We work eighty-hour weeks to prove our worth. Some of us emulate celebrities, dress in designer clothes, and drive expensive cars. We chase after dreams and ideas that were never meant for us.

The Bible says we're made in the image of *God*, in the very likeness of the Creator Himself. In Genesis 1:26, God says, "Let Us make man in Our image." When God created humankind, He gave us His own image—*imago Dei*. He created us in His own likeness, but knowingly or unknowingly, many of us have settled for terrible substitutes. We've created our own image by absorbing and reflecting the *culture* instead of letting God's image express itself through us.

And while we are doing all this striving, stretching, and straining to be *known*, to be *significant*, to be *understood* and *valued*, God looks down sadly shaking His head because He doesn't see children who resemble their Father. He doesn't see in us what we were designed to be.

But what is that? What does God expect to see?

God designed you in His image so that when He looks at you, it'll be like He's looking into a mirror. When He looks at you, He wants to see His glory reflected back to Him.

We've all heard the slogan "Image is everything." By redefining "image" as "our God IMAGE," that statement changes from a cultural cliché to a catchphrase of truth. This book has five sections, each one focusing on one aspect of our God IMAGE.

The IMAGE Journey

I've created an acrostic with the word *IMAGE*, and it looks like this:

I = Individually Unique

> You're unique, one of a kind. No one can take your place in God's universal design.

M = Moral Mirror

> You're created to reflect God's moral character, His heart, mind, and holiness.

A = Authority to Rule

> You've been empowered with the authority over your physical and spiritual environment, not people.

G = God's Friend

> You've been created to have, as a friend of God, an intimate, loving relationship with Him.

E = Eternal

> You've been designed to live forever with God.

Your image is more than an inscription or an imprint like you might see in a work of art or on a coin. Your God image goes much deeper; it goes to the very core of who you are. Your God image is alive and active, representing the invisible attributes of God living in your human design.

We're designed to actively pursue and reflect the glory of God through our lives. Like diamonds, we can only reflect the light that shines onto us; we have no twinkle of our own. The only light shining onto our image, our spiritual diamond, is the light of God's glory, which is projected onto us each and every day. So I go back to my original question. Do you know what God expects to see when He looks at you? What is He seeing right now?

Over 1,200 people were waiting for me to come out and talk to them. As the guards who brought me to this church were putting handcuffs on me, the knots in my stomach were getting worse. (These were the serial-killer, mass-murderer handcuffs that are attached to a chain that goes around your waist.) Less than a year before this particular Sunday, I was doing cocaine on the team plane. I was hanging out in crack houses and nightclubs. And I had turned down just about every speaking engagement that the team had offered me. So what was I doing telling a congregation about my experience in five prisons?

As they introduced me, the crowd got really quiet, and then I walked out. I began telling them how segregated prison is, with blacks, whites, and Hispanics hanging only with each other. I talked about the violence and code of ethics in prison. Then I introduced myself as a current defensive back with the San Diego Chargers.

There was no response. The people thought this inmate had lost his mind, and to be honest, I was just as shocked as they were. But the reason I had agreed to speak was really simple. I was beginning to realize that the direction my life had taken could not have been more opposite from my design. The God reflection that I was created to provide to God and to the world was beyond my wildest imagination, and I wanted to see that become a reality in my life.

I've written this book with the prayer that it will be an eye-opening journey to help you find and live the work of art God created you to be.

PART 1

INDIVIDUALLY UNIQUE

M
A
G
E

One of the most powerful reflections of God is seen in your individual uniqueness, the one-of-a-kind qualities with which you were created. There is no one like you in the entire world. God made you to reflect His creative genius.

Unfortunately, we have been deceived into marginalizing our individuality in order to fit into a dying and decaying world.

But thank God that He has provided us with the hope that the artistic genius that defines our individuality can be restored.

Chapters 1–4 will guide us through the process of understanding and restoring the brilliance of the "I" in our God IMAGE: our individuality!

1

Our Created Image

One of a Kind

The first was a picture of a girl with her hair blowing everywhere like a GoDaddy commercial. The second was a guy who looked like a beginner bodybuilder wearing WWF speedos and a Mr. T gold chain starter kit. The third picture was of a girl wearing a leopard bikini crawling on the floor and baring her teeth. These were the Facebook profile pictures of friends of one of my employees.

If you read a little further, you would learn their names, schools, jobs, favorite movies, and music. This is how people market themselves to friends, family, and the gazillions of Facebook users, saying, "Check me out, y'all."

What image do *you* want to project?

Certainly, your Facebook profile doesn't begin to capture the totality of the complex qualities that make up the truly amazing *you*. You're unique—not because of the music you like, the way you dress, or the talents you possess. Your race, culture, likes, dislikes, goals, dreams, and accomplishments don't identify or define the *real* you. Job applications, IQ and psychological tests, medical records, and bank statements don't define you either. All of these things may offer clues about your personality or your physical makeup, but they can't give us the sum total of who you are.

None of these characteristics or similarities will adequately describe the essence of your individuality, or what I refer to as the *I AM factor*.

Each of us is unique. There's absolutely no one like you or me in the entire world. God, who created us to be His children, has given us our own version of His I AM status, and it's the I AM factor. In this chapter you'll learn about how individually unique you are. You are not only different from other people but also from all other aspects of creation. I'll also outline how the characteristics of the I AM factor functions to produce a mirror *image* of God.

Your Individuality and the I AM Factor

As Moses is walking in the desert, he looks and sees a bush that is on fire but not burning. The fire is flowing around the branches of the bush, but the branches stay brown and the leaves remain green. When Moses gets up close to the bush, God speaks to him and tells him to go to Egypt and deliver the Jews from slavery.

Moses seems shocked. "Suppose I go to the Israelites and say to them, 'The God of your fathers has sent me to you,' and they ask me, 'What's His name?' What do I tell them?" Moses asks.

"I AM WHO I AM," God replies. "This is what you are to say to the Israelites. Tell them, I AM has sent you to them."

God is the great "I AM." This title refers to God's author-ity and supremacy as the Creator of all things. As the Great I AM, God exists independently. He relies on nothing else for His being. He is the source and the beginning of everything else. We possess a little of God's I AM-ness because we bear the image of God, which sets us apart from all other living things. No other creature bears God's image.

Listen to what David tells God in Psalm 139:13–15:

> You formed my inward parts;
> You covered me in my mother's womb.
> I will praise You, for I am fearfully and wonderfully
>   made;
> Marvelous are Your works,
> And that my soul knows very well.
> My frame was not hidden from You,
> When I was made in secret,
> And skillfully wrought in the lowest parts of the
>   earth.

You are marvelous. Why? Because there is no one else like you anywhere. Each one of us is unique, and we were created to provide the most complete mirror image of God on earth.

Reflecting the Glory of God

During my son's first month in the police academy, he brought home the biggest, baddest flashlight I'd ever seen. When I turned it on, a powerful beam of white light shot out of it. Like the light coming out of that flashlight, the invisible attributes of God are projected out of everything He has made and onto us with the expectation that the light or glory of His image will be reflected back to Him and to the world.

Romans 1:20 says, "For since the creation of the world His invisible attributes are clearly seen, being understood by the things that were made." What we see and experience all around us, in nature, for example, are expressions and evidence of the invisible attributes of God at work, such as wisdom, power, vision, creativity, organization, compassion, love, intelligence, and moral character. His invisible attributes are the basis of everything He does; they are part of everything He's made. Flowers exhibit God's artistic creativity. The sun demonstrates God's power. The stars in the sky declare His glory. The universe displays God's enormity, and the human cell shows God's infinite attention to detail.

We too reflect God's glory.

Our I AM factor—our individual uniqueness—positions us alone above all living things to recognize, appreciate, interpret, and interact with God's invisible attributes.

Uniquely Designed

Have you ever bit into a stick of celery and ended up with a bunch of strings stuck between your teeth? Those stringy things are called *xylem*. Like straws, they carry water and nutrients from the ground to each leaf on the celery plant. Just as the xylem plays an integral part in delivering life-sustaining nutrients to the celery, God designed our bodies as conduits for His invisible attributes to be expressed through us. Just as the xylem takes nutrients to the leaves, so our God image is expressed to others and the world through our bodies. God created our physical bodies as conduits for the spiritual nature of our God image.

Your physical makeup is a metaphor for the most powerful aspect of your "I AM factor." You and I are not people having spiritual experiences, but rather spirits in a human experience. God designed us to receive His spiritual input, then to use our physical body to reflect Him into the world. The spiritual aspect of our God image is the foundation of our God likeness and has the greatest potential of reflecting God. Romans 8:16 says, "The Spirit Himself bears witness with our spirit that we are children of God." We were designed to express the spiritual desires of God.

While walking through a park with my wife and children, I heard my wife and daughters say, "Oooh, look at the pretty flower." They began talking about how it smelled like a certain perfume and how the leaves felt like silk. They were able to recognize and appreciate the invisible attributes of God's creative design and sensitive heart in that created flower. God created you to appreciate beautiful, complex, and artistic things in a way unique to only you, and it is important to God that you express that unique perspective whenever you have the opportunity.

God gave you hands with five fingers so you can hold things for Him and provide His gentle touch. He gave you speech so you can mirror His words of compassion, love, and comfort. He gave you eyes to see what He sees. He gave you ears to listen on His behalf to the cries of the brokenhearted. God gave you a complex mind to reason, problem solve, dream, create, plan, engage in critical thinking, and make spiritual decisions, like He does. He gave you a heart to reflect His love to a broken world.

You have the ability to feel and reflect His emotions of compassion, joy, encouragement, and empathy because that is how God created you. As God's glory is projected onto you, He actively *showers* you with His invisible attributes, such as love, wisdom, and creativity, so you will reflect all this back to Him and to the world.

Uniquely Creative

While on vacation in the Caribbean, my daughter and I decided to go kayaking in the ocean. Every five minutes or so we'd stop, put on our face masks, and lower our faces into the water to look for fish. After about thirty minutes of paddling, we found ourselves in forty feet of water and decided it was a good time to look for fish. This time my daughter's mask fell off her face. As soon as I jumped in the water to get it, the undercurrent swept me thirty to forty feet away. It felt like the offensive line of the Raiders was pushing me farther and farther away from her.

I started to panic a bit, and then things got worse. Jellyfish. Plural. Think of 100 needles jabbing your whole body. Now make that 100 red-hot needles. People have died from an allergic reaction to jellyfish stings. Now I'm feeling my body start to seriously burn, and the waves are dunking me. I can see the look of sheer terror on my daughter's face as she continued to drift away from me. I was praying all the way, "Lord, please, get me back to my baby girl."

I finally made it to the kayak and began to paddle back to shore. I prayed that I wouldn't have a terrible allergic reaction to the stings. I paddled for at least half an hour, and the whole time my eyes hurt worse and became more and more watery, my body throbbed and burned as though on fire, and all I could think of was to pray, "God, please get us back to the beach."

When at last we got to shore, there was a dead jellyfish lying at the water's edge, and I wanted so bad to do the River Dance on his head because of what his cousins did to me, but instead I had to give it some respect. Jellyfish have been known to kill people, yet they have no brains, no blood, and no bones. They are 90 percent water! How can something made mostly of water almost take me out?

God's creativity is off the chart. Did you know there's a flea that can jump its own height multiplied hundreds of times? It would be like you or me jumping two Empire State buildings! God created an ant that can carry thirty-five times its weight on its own back. God designed fish with lights on top of their heads so they can see in the dark. God created the polar bear to gain nearly four hundred pounds during pregnancy and give birth while sleeping. God designed wasps so they can recognize each other's faces, giving them the ability to defend their own families against enemy wasps. Other animals recognize and/or communicate with each other by smell or sound or vibration on land or in water.

God created seemingly endless categories of animals that crawl on the ground, fly in the sky, swim in the ocean, and live beneath the earth's surface. He created species with their own unique patterns, shapes, sizes, and colors. Scientists have named and cataloged 1.3 million species of animals. There are approximately 20,000 classifications of roses and over 10,000 species of birds in the world. There are 2,700 snake species, 7,000 varieties of apples, 12,000 to 20,000 types of butterflies, and 150,000 to 250,000 moth types. Every leaf can be traced back to an individual tree, and every plant is distinguished by its own unique DNA.

What I find interesting is that each year we continue to discover, name, and categorize more animals and plants, just like Adam did in Genesis (see vv. 19–20, 23). The naming and categorizing of the animals and plants is unique to us as humans and another facet of our ability to echo God's image. God not only designed you with complex and advanced capabilities, He also made you to interact with Him and His unlimited creativity. You were designed to recognize, acknowledge, and glorify God's creativity.

Uniquely Free

One summer day I was sitting in my house with my windows open when I heard my neighbor's two dogs howling and barking at the top of their lungs. As I listened, I realized the dogs had escaped. One dog was a beagle, a type of hound, and the other was a mutt.

The beagle had caught scent of something, and his hound instincts took over—he was hunting something down. He ran back and forth from the fence to the street lamp to the bushes, trying to find the animal that had left the scent.

The mutt, on the other hand, had no idea what was going on, so she just barked. I could almost hear her saying something like, "Where are we going? Why are we barking? What are we looking for?" The beagle, however, was on a mission.

Animals seem to have a robotic quality; their patterns are predictable. They have certain times when they mate, other times when they migrate—for the most part, animals spend their lives looking for food, mating, protecting territory, and sleeping. Humans, on the other hand, have the ability to make many more, sometimes unpredictable, choices about these activities.

Animals establish strict territories where they live, but you and I are free to create and explore the sky, the sea, and space, and develop new means of habitation throughout the world.

You are free to be the creative person God made you to be. You are able to study and learn science, medicine, and law; invent new technology; build cities; and develop various music styles and genres of writing. You are free to create wondrous forms of art, to take the colors God has given and make new hues and patterns. You are free to build sand castles, play sports, develop countless games to play; try out new and creative ways of teaching and learning; develop medical advances and cures for disease. You are free to help preserve wildlife and feed hungry people around the world. God has made you in His image in part so you can leave this world a better place.

Why is that so marvelous? Because you have been patterned after your Creator. Do you feel that you are using and developing and investing in the creativity God has given you? Our culture places so much pressure on people to fit in and conform that we can lose the freedom God has given us to be uniquely creative. God's intention is for you to develop your full potential.

Individually You

While you are distinguished from all other living things, you are also unlike any other *person*. Currently there are seven billion people on earth, and not *one* of these seven billion looks just like you! And what you look like is only the *beginning* of your uniqueness.

I recently noticed a black mole just above my lip. I thought I was going crazy, thinking that I didn't know my own face. Now I call it my Cindy Crawford. Take a minute and look in the mirror. Your facial expressions are all yours, exclusive to you alone. There is no one with your lips, eyes, eyebrows, freckles, goofy ears, and crooked tooth.

You also have your own heartbeat rhythm and your very own fragrance or funky smell. No one has your voice, fingerprints, and footprints. No other person carries your resourcefulness, perspective, and values.

Can you see now how absolutely amazing and marvelous you are?

Individually Purposed and Promised

Whenever I go to the doctor for a physical, I ask questions about every part of the exam. I'm fascinated by all the instruments they use to perform the physical, and without fail I end up asking the doctor to let me use those instruments on him. Because my doctor is pretty cool, he usually lets me look in his eyes, down his throat, in his ears. He lets me listen to his heart and tap on his knee. He explains to me how each of the instruments works. He explains how they're designed and how each one is intended to be used and handled. Each one of his instruments was designed for a very specific purpose.

In the same way, God has specific purposes for all of His children. God has a very specific and unique purpose for how He wants you to reflect His attributes to the world. Jeremiah's words to the Israelites in exile in Babylon are also appropriate for us today. He says in Jeremiah 29:11, "I know the plans I have for you, declares the LORD, plans for welfare and not for evil, to give you a future and a hope" (ESV).

If you are true to the uniqueness of how God designed you, it isn't possible for you to have a life identical to anyone else's. In order for God to be seen and known on earth, He created billions of unique individuals who can express very specific aspects of who He is.

> God has a very specific and unique purpose for how He wants you to reflect His attributes to the world.

Your purpose is important, intentional, and God ordained. Consequently, God has made very specific promises and commitments just to *you*. He's designed you to fulfill your unique purpose in life. He created you to stand out as one of a kind—unlike anyone on earth—so please stop trying to fit in and be like everyone else. You're not like everyone else. God is equipping and preparing you to live an individual and unique life, reflecting the aspects of God that you were ordained to reflect.

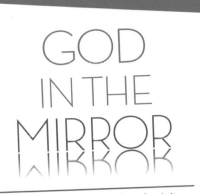

GOD IN THE MIRROR

Help others **SEE** God in the Mirror

GOD IN THE MIRROR CHALLENGE

1. **Read through the book**
   • Then give to a friend to read

2. **Promote & Share:**
   • Post a picture with the book and share what you are learning. Include the link: *bit.ly/godinthemirror* & use #GodInTheMirror through social media:

   • Write a review on Amazon *bit.ly/godinthemirror* & purchase for a friend

3. **Join a GITM Community Group:** *sdrock.com/GITM*

4. **Enjoy free resources at** *milesmcpherson.com/godinthemirror*

mage

oster

vith the precision of a
page on the pavement,
a muddy French fry, a
s open the packet with
ike soda. The creature
d with grease. It grunts
chews, and swallows.
f an abandoned build-
pared to pounce but as
eps sucking on a piece
dawn it lies trembling
lize this is no animal.

on the streets and al-
rld. He's hovering in
nfested blankets. He's

23

panhandling on freeway entrances. In some countries he is born and dies on the streets.

Is this beat-up and broken-down scavenger on the streets created in the image of God and as full of potential as you are? Is he born to be as amazing as you are? What do you think?

Yes, he is. Absolutely, most definitely yes. He, you, and I all possess the *imago Dei* from God.

But how does a person created in God's image wind up covered in dirt and curled up asleep in a doorway like a dog? We could blame his family, the neighborhood he grew up in, the economy, or his teachers, but the root of all self-destruction doesn't *originate* from any of these. This same self-destruction can and does happen to all of us to some degree, so pay attention to see how much of this applies to you. How does the business executive who drives a Mercedes and owns his own house begin thinking it is because of his intelligence and hard work only that he enjoys the nice things of life? How does the soccer mom or schoolteacher or nurse lie in bed each night thinking that she is a good person, so good enough and deserving of the blessing of God that she would look down on the poor? The root is an evil so deceptively powerful and wicked that not one living thing on earth can resist it.

You are amazing, created in God's image, and your individual uniqueness and creativity possess unlimited potential. Unfortunately, many of us will never experience the full potential of our individuality because we have turned our back on our true selves, the person we were created to be. We have sold ourselves out by trying to be someone we are not. Have you fallen for the oldest trick in the book and tried to become your own god?

In this chapter we'll focus on how our I AM factor is converted to an *I AM imposter* and how that new identity will lead to self-destruction.

How does someone who's been created in the eternal, glorious image of God turn into a derelict, a drug addict, or a self-centered, deceitful person? Why do people with the potential to change the world end up failing at everything but destruction? How does a person turn the amazing creation of God into something from the pit of hell? Self-destruction!

Satan's Number One Weapon

One of my first speaking engagements in youth ministry was in Philadelphia. The day before I spoke, I read about a huge flea market being held in the parking lot outside the Veterans Stadium where the Philadelphia Eagles played at the time. My imagination drew a picture of a different kind of flea market, one where everything was *free* . . .

Hundreds of booths surround the stadium, and cars have come from all over Pennsylvania, New Jersey, Delaware, and upstate New York. Traffic is jammed with pickup trucks, semis, and SUVs. People are filling their vehicles as fast as they can grab stuff.

On top of the stadium, the devil sits, laughing at his flea market. He has a panoramic view of it all as the people grab everything. His demons are giving away packages of disease, booklets on suicide, boxes and boxes of porn, murder, and adultery.

As the devil stands on the edge of the stadium, pointing over the parking lot, he sneers and says, "Just look at all these fools, they actually think this stuff is going to make them happy. Little do they know that it's gonna destroy them. They have seen what this stuff does to people, but they are dumb enough to believe that it won't happen to them."

Satan runs flea markets everywhere—in alleys, in crack houses, in your home through your computer. And some of his "merchandise" is disguised as things we think are good, like making a lot of money, or succeeding in our job, or even fighting for the rights of others.

How does the devil get people to destroy themselves? Satan can't *make* anybody destroy their life, he can only deceive them into sin. His biggest weapon comes in two parts. I'll deal with the first one in this chapter and the second in chapter 6.

Before we get to that, though, let's talk about the reality of the devil. Some people may claim they don't believe in the devil, but they sure know evil when they see it. One night my wife and I took our kids to the movies. Just before the movie began, they showed previews of the new exorcist movie. This new movie took Creepy Freaky Scary to another level. The possessed girl's fingers snapped sideways, she crawled on the ceiling and howled like an animal. Of course, there was blood everywhere. The hair on my arms stood up, and as soon as the preview ended, someone in the front row yelled out, "JESUS!" The entire crowd started laughing, the kind of laughter that acknowledges that something good needed to replace the evil that had filled the theater—an evil that could be felt.

Satan is evil personified. He's the mastermind of murder and rape. He's the designer of child molestation and abuse. He's the one who motivates and inspires the plans of a serial killer. The devil is the instigator of every evil and perverted act. He can't create anything, but he perverts what God has created for good.

A major deceptive device of Satan's diabolical plan is to get us to destroy God's image in us. Satan hates God and everything He stands for. Satan once was one of God's most beautiful angels until he rebelled against God and was kicked out of heaven. Pride and ambition can't exist in heaven, where all things are holy and perfect like God, so Satan and his pride fell from God's presence and a third of the angels fell with him. Those fallen angels became demons. Ever since that day, Satan has been working overtime to destroy God's most beloved creation: *people*. It makes perfect sense that since he can't destroy God, he attacks the next best thing: those made in God's image with the intent to remind the world of the greatness and goodness of God. That's what you represent. Whether you know it or like it, because you were created for good, you are a target of evil.

Remember, Satan can't destroy you without your participation. At some point you must work with him in your self-destruction before he can change what God created you to have and be. In order to turn you from your amazing individual and uniquely created self as God intended into a creature eating spiritual garbage, Satan needs your approval. But how does he get it? What is Satan's number one weapon? It comes in two parts, the second to be covered in chapter 6.

Satan's Weapon, Part One: Becoming Your Own God

When God created you in His image, He gave you the awareness of your individual uniqueness. He gave you a creative mind and the freedom to be creative and to recognize creativity. He created you to walk in unity with the original intent of His image. He designed you to enjoy His love and majesty, as long as you live consistent with His plan for your life. You are intended to fulfill the uniqueness and creativity of your individual design.

Included in that design is the freedom to choose to obey God, and *this* is what Satan takes advantage of: your *freedom of choice*. He wants to rob you of your individual identity. Satan knows you were made with an active spiritual and physical ability to reflect the glory of God, like a mirror. He's aware of the living nature of God's image in you. He knows that if he can get you disconnected from depending on God, he can redirect your mind any way he wants. He can influence your passion and your efforts to glorify *yourself* instead of God. This is all an attempt to redefine who you are.

Satan knows self-glorification is the fastest and most direct path to self-destruction, because it is what destroyed him. The devil wants you to think that you can do what you want and, therefore, you can be like God—in control of your own life and independent of Him.

> Satan wants to rob you of your individual identity.

In Genesis 3, Satan slid over to Eve and said, "Hey girl, what's your name?"

Flinging her hair back, she said, "Eve."

"Did God really say you couldn't eat from every tree in the garden? C'mon, girl, you don't believe that, do you? You won't die, but you will be like God, knowing good and evil on your own."

Convincing you that you can be like God and make decisions on your own without God's direction and help is part one of Satan's number one weapon. He wants you to think that you don't need the Great I AM, that you can be your own I AM, but you'll just end up an I AM imposter.

The I AM Imposter

Satan's plan is to turn God's image in you against God Himself by turning you into an I AM imposter. An I AM imposter is someone who has become his or her own god. Once the devil tricks you into changing your identity to be your own god, you'll start to think you can do fine without God, and that'll be the beginning of your self-destruction.

The very strengths of your God image will be directed at serving yourself, and you'll implode. Since you're now an I AM imposter, the devil will entice you to think you can run your life on your own terms and do whatever you feel like doing. You determine right and wrong, not anyone else. Not even God.

Satan whispers in your ear, "You don't need to be bound by the Bible. You don't need to listen to that preacher. You don't need to go to church or pray. Who needs all that? Since you are now Mr. Big Stuff, you're just fine on your own. You've got everything under control."

I used to think that I could use drugs and that it would not negatively affect or destroy me like it did others. Then during a physical with the San Diego Chargers, the doctor looked in my nose and asked me if I had been using cocaine. How could he know that? My heart started pounding in my chest, and I thought I was going to get cut that day. The doc knew I was using because the cocaine had eaten away at the inside of my nose.

Your sin will always find you out. If you think that you can beat the devil at his own game, he's got you fooled. There is no way you can abuse what God has given you and not pay a price.

Proving Your Significance

Once you have adopted Satan's identity for yourself apart from God, you have to validate that identity by *proving* your value and importance. You become chained to earning acceptance and approval, always working to *be* something, to make something of yourself. The devil will be right in your face challenging your identity, like he challenged Jesus by demanding He prove Himself in Matthew 4: "If you're the Son of God, prove it! Do this, if you are the Son of God, do that." The devil will confront you in the same way. "If you're cool, wear this! If you're a player, sleep with her! If you've got money, buy that! If you're so smart, brag about your grades! If you're cute, wiggle the jiggle and show it off!"

You could spend a lot of years manipulating people or fooling yourself into being a little god, an I AM imposter, whatever he has convinced you to be. What a waste of time. Would you agree that Satan has been successful in wearing you out trying to prove yourself, to be someone that God never intended you to be? I know people who spend their entire lives trying to fulfill someone else's vision or expectations for their lives, when in fact they would have been so much more fulfilled sticking to God's plan for them.

If you fall for his game, it could land you in jail, a rehab center, divorce court, bankruptcy court, a garbage can, or sleeping in doorways. Satan can drive you crazy and run you through a maze of failure, and then one day you'll die having missed the biggest opportunity you ever had, which was fulfilling the unlimited potential of reflecting God's image to the world.

Head Game

There was a lady who shopped at a certain grocery store where the owner had a parrot. Every time the lady passed the parrot in its cage, it squawked, "Stupid lady! Stupid lady!" The first time she heard the parrot, she ignored it. But then later at the exit the parrot squawked at her again, "Stupid lady! Stupid lady!" This happened every week, so after about three trips to the grocery store she approached the manager and told him what the parrot said to her.

"He always calls out, 'Stupid lady, stupid lady' when he sees me!" she complained.

Flustered and embarrassed, the manager apologized for the behavior of the parrot and assured her it would not call her stupid again.

A week later the woman went to buy her groceries, thinking, "That parrot better not call me stupid lady, he better not call me stupid lady." While she shopped, she thought, "He better not call me stupid lady, he better not call me stupid lady." When she approached the cash register, she kept telling herself, "He better not call me stupid lady. He better not call me stupid lady." She paid for her groceries, thinking, "He better not call me stupid lady." She couldn't get "Stupid lady! Stupid lady!" out of her head. She was a nervous wreck by the time she was ready to leave the store. The parrot sat in its cage casually watching her, and as she got closer and closer, the parrot just stared at her. She got right up to the cage and she looked at the parrot, and the parrot looked at her and said, "You know!"

The devil can get into your head so deep that you'll be convinced you're a failure, a loser, stupid, or whatever name or curse he has attached to your new godless identity. How deep has Satan gotten into your head? What lies about yourself have enslaved you and prevented you from becoming the unique and marvelous person God created you to be?

Lie or Truth

Here's a comparison between your I AM factor and the characteristics God intended for your identity, and those associated with an I AM imposter identity. God intended for you to rest in who He made you to be. Satan's identity will result in nothing but restlessness and unnecessary striving.

God's truth to His image bearers:	The devil's lies to everyone:
You're My *success*. (Josh. 1:8)	You're a failure.
You're My *winner*. (Phil. 3:13–14)	You're a loser.
You're *unique* in My family. (Ps. 139:12–14)	You're better than others.

God's truth to His image bearers:	The devil's lies to everyone:
You're filled with My *promises*. (Heb. 6:12)	You're hopeless.
You can do *all things* through Me. (Phil. 4:13)	You can't do anything right.
I am the Lord who *heals you*. (Ps. 103:3)	You'll always be weak and sick.
You are born for "*such a time as this*." (Esther 4:14) And will *long enjoy* the work of your hands.(Isa. 65:22)	You don't get the breaks others do.
Everything under heaven is Mine. (Job 41:11)	I can give you the world!
You're *loved* with an everlasting love. (Jer. 31:3)	Nobody loves you.

My prayer is that God opens your eyes and reveals to you who you are and where your life is going so you will not allow it to be destroyed by Satan's lies.

3

Return of the I AM

Hand-in-Glove

When I was a kid growing up in New York, the first thing that came to mind when it snowed was a snowball fight. If there was enough snow, the next most important thing was having a good pair of gloves. Those mitten things were horrible for snowball fights. Good-fitting, five-finger gloves were critical for forming tight snowballs and hitting your friend upside his head even if he was hiding behind a tree. We'd never do well in a snowball fight if our gloves got all crusty with ice or if they fell off every time we threw; and if the gloves were too small or had holes in them, we'd end up with frozen fingers. The best gloves had to fit so perfectly on your hands that they were one with your hand, an extension of your skin.

God created you in His image so He, through His Spirit, can fit snug inside you, like a hand in a well-fitting glove—not too loose and not too tight, but just right. Think of your five fingers as the five ways you reflect God's image to the world: your *individual uniqueness*, your *moral mirror*, your *authority to rule*, your position as *God's friend*, and your *eternal spirit*. With God living inside you like fingers in a glove, He'll restore you to your full potential. In this chapter we'll focus on how Jesus *restores* your uniqueness, your I AM factor.

Running in the Wrong Direction?

When I entered my fourth year with the San Diego Chargers, we drafted four rookie defensive backs. One of them was arguably the fastest guy on the team, but because he was a rookie, he'd often get confused and run the wrong direction! It is hard to win when the fastest guy on the team is running the wrong way.

You may be running fast, making business deals, dating this person or that person, going to this party, and hanging with so and so, but what good does it do you if you're running in the wrong direction?

Living as a blurred image, disconnected from God and His Word, pulls us away from God faster than we can manage to resist. Every spiritual offense separates us from Him and results in spiritual death.

A glove without a hand in it is nothing more than material in the shape of a hand. Nothing inside, no life. The glove can't do anything without a living hand inside it. It is useless.

Remember, being a spiritually dead person doesn't mean you can't walk, talk, build a family, or run a business, but it does mean that your activity isn't glorifying God on a spiritual level. It means that your actions, thoughts, and intentions are not initiated or driven by God. It is all about you, the fake God, the I AM imposter. If the image of God in you isn't activated by your faith and the power of God, you're bound to end up running in the wrong direction, serving yourself, and doing wrong as if it were right.

You can't fix your blurred God image on your own. You cannot regain your original God-given identity on your own. You need a savior with a unique skill set. *Jesus is that One.* He's the Savior uniquely qualified and positioned to restore your spiritual life to what God had in mind when He created you.

The Unique One

Your individual uniqueness described in chapter 1 of this book is fulfilled and restored when you surrender and submit yourself to Jesus, the Unique Perfect One. His title as the only begotten Son (John 3:16) literally means "one of a kind, unique." Jesus is "the one and only Son of God."

But before He can bring us back to life through the process of restoring God's image in us, He must deliver us from death.

God created us in His image with the intent that we would live a fulfilling life. In turn, we ruined that opportunity by turning our backs on Him, so He sent Jesus to pay the price for us turning away from God and to restore our God image to its full potential. What are you going to do with that opportunity?

Two Ways to Heaven?

In the middle of a conversation about God with a guy on a plane, I was asked if I believed there was only one way to heaven. The guy was convinced, in light of all the religions in the world, that there had to be many ways to get to God and was banking on me arguing to the contrary with him. He was ready to hit me with his "We all just need to get along" speech, and that's when I dropped the bomb on him.

I said there were actually *two* ways to get to heaven. Then I paused to let that sink in, because I knew I had just rocked his world. Maybe yours too. One of the most common arguments against Christianity is that people can't accept the thought of a religious leader named Jesus who lived 2,000 years ago as the only way to heaven. When I told the guy that there were actually two ways to get to heaven, he froze where he sat, with his mouth open. I didn't do or say anything. I like to let those things marinate a little. I wanted it to sizzle his brain for a few seconds.

I broke the silence with a soft voice and told him that one way to heaven is to live a perfect life as a perfect mirror image of God, inside and out, and then you can VIP yourself right through the gates. But if you're not perfect inside and out, you can get someone to stand in for you, someone who *is* a perfect mirror image of God to pay the death penalty you owe for your sins. Once this perfect image of God pays the price for your sins, He will live inside your image, like a hand in a glove, and begin to move the fingers of the glove in the way they were originally created to move.

The dude just sat there, mouth still open.

We have to keep in mind that heaven is a place for those who perfectly reflect God's character, glory, and love! The only way God is going to see Himself in us on this side of heaven is if *He Himself* lives in us. The only way He sees Himself in our actions and the intentions of our hearts is if *He Himself* fits in us like a hand in a glove, empowering us and giving us direction.

When Jesus died on the cross, He did what only He was equipped and positioned to do: pay the death penalty that we owe God. Because sin is a spiritual offense, the restoration—the payment—needs to be spiritual as well. Jesus is the sinless Savior who came to earth voluntarily to become the sacrifice for us. He was cruelly rejected and killed at the hands of those He came to save and restore. He died a gruesome death as the final sacrifice for us, and it's through Him that we're saved from the hopelessness we've created in our lives. We need someone perfect, someone flawless, to stand in our place, and that's what Jesus did for us on the cross. But His death and resurrection does us no good unless we accept His ultimate sacrifice as payment for our sins.

I know that for many of you this is not new information, so here is your Christianity 101 challenge question. When was the last time you shared this information with someone? I am not talking about drive-by witnessing where you shoot out a few gospel truths, and before anyone can act on it, you are gone. Let me ask the question a different way: When was the last time you actually led someone to the Lord?

In John 3 a religious leader named Nicodemus came to Jesus at night for a talk about God and the promised Messiah. Jesus told him the words that have confused many minds: "Unless one is born again, he cannot see the kingdom of God" (v. 3). Nicodemus asked how he could go back into his mother a second time. What Jesus meant is that we must be *spiritually* born. If your earthly parents are those people through whom your natural birth occurred, it makes sense that your spiritual Father would be the one through whom your *spiritual* birth occurs.

When you're born again, a dramatic and radical change happens with your fallen nature. You hand over to God your blurred image and He gives you back a clean, polished, new, born-again self that reflects His image in the way that He always intended. Jesus the Savior saves us from ourselves! He saves us from the rebellious desires that come from being disconnected from God. Once you've accepted His forgiveness, He comes and lives in you like a hand inside a glove.

It is then that we become new creations. You don't do anything except say *yes* to receive this new life, just like you didn't do anything to bring about your natural birth.

To be *born again* is a gift of grace.

Now, on a daily basis you need to make the conscious choice to turn from a self-guided life to a God-filled life and to allow Jesus the Lord to be everything in your life.

When Jesus died and rose from the dead, He made a promise to send His Holy Spirit to live in us. "I will pray the Father, and He will give you another Helper, that He may abide with you forever—the Spirit of truth, whom the world cannot receive, because it neither sees Him nor knows Him; but you know Him, for He dwells with you and will be in you" (John 14:16–17).

> We're spiritual beings having a human experience, not human beings having a spiritual experience.

It's the work of the Holy Spirit interacting with the image of God in you that restores you back to what God originally intended you to be and reflects God's glory. The Holy Spirit guides and directs you to operate in the way God created you. We're spiritual beings having a human experience, not human beings having a spiritual experience.

The Holy Spirit will convict you of your sin, pray on your behalf, remind you of the Word of God, and stir your heart how to act. This ongoing restoration is what gives us eternal hope. Colossians 1:27 says that *Christ in us* is the hope of glory. The presence of the work of Christ in our lives gives us hope that we can be restored and that God will begin to see Himself in us as clearly as if He were looking in a mirror. It's in the context of our *ongoing* dependence on God that our hope is restored through the day-to-day expression of Christ *through* us. We learn over time to depend on the guidance of the Holy Spirit to live a life that resembles the glory of God.

I can't tell you how many times I have been asked how I know God is speaking to me. Well, God in the form of the Holy Spirit speaks with a small voice that sounds like our conscience. The only difference is that He is telling us things that are always agreeable with the Bible and the character of God. The key is to obey that voice. That is what it means to be guided or led by the Spirit of God.

Return of the I AM

Jesus fought constantly with the religious critics. They were regularly trying to catch Him contradicting Old Testament law. In John 8:56–59, there's an account of these critics thinking they caught Him contradicting Himself. The scene goes like this:

JESUS: Your father Abraham rejoiced that he would see my day. He saw it and was glad.

PHARISEES: You are not yet fifty years old, and have you seen Abraham?

JESUS: Truly, truly, I say to you, before Abraham was, I AM.

The Pharisees went postal and picked up stones to throw at Him, but Jesus calmly walked out of the temple.

The reason the Pharisees reacted this way is because Jesus equated Himself to the "I AM"—God Himself—who spoke to Moses in the desert 1,400 years earlier. They thought that Jesus was claiming to be God, which He was! "I and My Father are one" (John 10:30).

Jesus tried to get through to them that *He* is the I AM. He's telling you the same thing. Your I AM factor, your individual uniqueness, will be restored, renewed, and nurtured when the "I AM" Himself, Jesus Christ, makes *His* home in your heart.

Think of salvation as the surrender of your *imago Dei* back to God and the process of restoring God's image in you to function in the way God originally intended. The more His image is restored in you, the more drama you avoid, and the more drama you can help others avoid. They'll see God alive and well in you. They'll see the new you, and this will generate hope that they too will be delivered from spiritual doom.

As the only begotten Son, Jesus restores our uniqueness.

As the living Word of Truth, Jesus restores God's morality into our character.

As the possessor of all authority in heaven and earth, Jesus restores the authority He originally gave us.

As the Son, He redeems a powerful and secure relationship with the Father and prepares us to enjoy that relationship into eternity.

As the risen Savior, He ensures that we can have eternal life.

Jesus replaces the division caused by the blurred image of God in us. He does this by reestablishing us as one with the Father, as He is.

One with the Father

When we live in a way that is consistent with the image of God in us, we're living in unity with God—we're *one* with God in purpose and thought. Satan works overtime to cause division between God and us. Jesus came to us to make us *one with the Father*, to reunite us permanently with Him. He prayed:

> And the glory which You gave Me I have given them, *that they* may *be one* just as We are *one*: I in them, and You in Me; *that they* may *be* made perfect in *one*, and *that* the world may know *that* You have sent Me, and have loved them as You have loved Me. Father, I desire that they also whom You gave Me may be with Me where I am, that they may behold My glory which You have given Me; for You loved Me before the foundation of the world. (John 17:22–24)

You're now free to *totally become* the unique you that you were born to be. You're free to be you and do what you were meant to do for the glory of God.

This is not a religious relationship but a *spiritual union*. It empowers everything unique about you. You've been re-created as a unique individual with Christ alive in you by His Spirit, and you're now one with your Creator.

The Bible says you have "the mind of Christ" (1 Cor. 2:16)! You have all the qualities of Jesus that He possessed while on earth, not only making you unique, but also equipping you to express that uniqueness to the world.

A Unique Name and a Unique Relationship

In my neighborhood growing up, practically everyone was called by at least two names. The first name was the one our parents gave us, and the second was a name the neighborhood gave us. One of my friends named Vance was also called Heavy because he weighed maybe 350 pounds. We called Tyrone T-Rock because he was the muscle in our crowd. Jerome was called Pop, and I'll never know why. Another brother named Jack was called Black Jack because he was, well, really black.

When Jesus comes to live in your heart, He gives you another name, one in addition to the name your parents gave you. He calls you *Christian*, and He has a few more. He calls you *Child of God, Victor, Conqueror, Beloved, Saint*.

The uniqueness that Christ offers you is *personal*. He speaks to you *individually* and *personally*. He calls you to Himself in a voice and manner meant just for you. He speaks directly into your heart so you can hear Him. "My sheep hear My voice, and I know them, and they follow Me" (John 10:27).

The love of the Holy Spirit has been drawing you to your Father your whole life because He wants a unique relationship with you. He wants to speak to you, to bless you, and to guide you.

A New Heart and a New Reflection

God spoke to the prophet Ezekiel about faith in a Messiah with these words: "I will give you *a new heart* and put a new spirit within you; I will take the *heart* of stone out of your flesh and give you a *heart* of flesh" (Ezek. 36:26).

Paul said in 2 Corinthians 5:17 that "if anyone is in Christ, he is a new creation; old things have passed away; behold, all things have become new." This is the new heart and the new life that faith in God brings.

Once you've said yes to Jesus, you've become a new person.

When God looks at Jesus, He sees Himself reflected back because they're One. With Jesus living in our hearts, God looks at us and sees Jesus's victory on the cross, and He sees our sins forgiven. *God sees us through His Son.* If that sounds incredible, remember Jesus's words of John 14:9: "He who has seen Me has seen the Father."

Adopted

We're uniquely adopted into God's family. Look at Romans 8:15–17:

> For you did not receive the spirit of bondage again to fear, but you received the Spirit of adoption by whom we cry out, "Abba, Father." The Spirit Himself bears witness with our spirit that we are children of God, and if children, then heirs—heirs of God and joint heirs with Christ.

Welcome home.

4

The Image Magnifier

Uniquely Unique

My youngest brother, Don, was an All-American NCAA Division I football player for Syracuse University. As quarterback he led the nation in passing and was the runner-up for the 1987 Heisman trophy award. From time to time my brother runs into former teammates who are all doing interesting things with their lives. One of them is Jeff Mangram, who played cornerback for the Syracuse Orangemen. After a little preliminary small talk, my brother asked him what he was doing, and Jeff said that, in addition to having a PhD and being a professor at Syracuse, he was teaching gifted students in a local private school. My brother didn't remember Jeff being the brainy type, so he was scratching his head and stuttering in surprise. He asked Jeff again, "What did you say you were doing?" Jeff realized that my brother was a little confused and understood why. He spontaneously pounded on his chest and yelled, "I'm gifted, and I never knew it!"

You are a gifted person, and you need to *know* it. You are a one of a kind individually unique creative wonder.

There's absolutely *no one* who can do what *you* can do in the way God has designed for *you* to do it. The combination of your personality, your experience, and the Holy Spirit's work in your life are very special tools that can be of great use in the kingdom of God. God considers your gifts extremely valuable. He goes before you and leads you to the people He intends for your life to touch.

The church, as our image magnifier, is meant to provide a place for the image of God in you to grow, develop, and function at its highest level. In this chapter I am going to focus on how the church helps magnify your ability to reflect the image of God and on the important role *your individuality* plays in empowering the church to fulfill its role in building the kingdom of God.

The Body

The body has sixty trillion cells, all of which have one million pages of information inside the cell's DNA. Even though each cell has the same exact information in it, each one performs individually unique functions to make up bone cells, muscle cells, blood cells, skin cells, heart cells, and more. These cells are all different because they are accessing a different portion of information from your DNA. Not only does your DNA tell your cells what kind of cell to be, it groups cells together to form organs and other body parts, then it instructs the organs about how to function with each other.

Each cell finds its fullest value when it becomes the unique cell it's designed to be with its unique function and when it fulfills its unique function in partnership with the other parts of the body. If your cells fail to work in partnership with the other cells, your body won't operate properly. Cells that function independently from or inconsistently with their design are sometimes called cancer. In other words, if your body is to function well, each of your sixty trillion cells must cooperate, coordinate, and *work together at the direction of your DNA*.

The church, called the *body of Christ*, functions the same way our physical body works, but on a spiritual level. Just as your body consists of sixty trillion complex cells, each one directed by the information based in the DNA of the nucleus of the cell, so the collective group of believers make up the body of Christ, each one directed by the Holy Spirit in their heart. The Bible says that the body should "grow up in all things into Him who is the head—Christ—from whom the whole body, joined and knit together by what every joint supplies, according to the effective working by which every part does its share, causes growth of the body for the edifying of itself in love" (Eph. 4:15–16).

The body of Christ, the church, can't function at its most efficient level unless each individual person utilizes his or her unique talents and gifts in the way God intended them to be utilized. We experience and become the best unique version of ourselves when we live in a collaborative relationship with a community of believers. We must view church as much more than just a place to hear a sermon on Sunday. One of the church's purposes is to provide an opportunity for our individual unique role in God's kingdom to be developed and used.

The Handicapped Church?

During my rookie season in the NFL, I had the privilege of volunteering for the Special Olympics. It was inspiring to see the contestants running, jumping, and competing even though they were hindered by all kinds of handicaps and disabilities. They were obviously so determined and passionate that I wondered what they could have done had they not been disabled.

Sometimes the body of Christ behaves as though it's handicapped. It is trying to run on crutches or operate in wheelchairs. It acts like it can't hear or see. If the church is the body of Christ, why is it limping along like it has no legs? Jesus is not handicapped; He's fully able to do the impossible. Why does His body sometimes act like it can't see His vision for the world? Why is His body deaf to His voice? Ephesians 2:10 says that God has equipped each person (and consequently His church) for every good work. This means there is no trial we can't face and overcome as a body of believers.

There are enough people gifted with the Holy Spirit in the church to change the world, but all too often God's children are preoccupied by their jobs, or they're leading busy lives and unwilling to volunteer their time to help others with the gifts God has given them. There's enough money in the churches to fulfill every expense God sends its way—the only problem is that the money is in the bank accounts of the people. God projects His patience and His grace on the church, so it is *more* than equipped to stand strong and has *more* than enough resources to be a clear reflection of His love for the world.

When you walk into church, you bring with you your unique talents and abilities, and God has a special assignment for each one of you. Some people think of church as a Sunday event for the benefit of the people in their seats. There's truth to that, of course, but what's often overlooked is where the benefit is to come from. *You!*

Jeff, mentioned at the beginning of this chapter, uses his unique gift to help gifted kids learn. You and I need to look for opportunities to use our gifts to help people—*the people who are sitting right next to us in church.* When you identify and exercise your individual gifts, you'll bless someone whose unique need matches your unique gift.

After church one Sunday a woman came up to me crying about the divorce she was going through. I prayed with her and then referred her to a ministry for women dealing with the pain of divorce that my former secretary started after her own difficult marriage. A man who was addicted to porn came to me for prayer, and I was able to refer him to a ministry for men with sex addictions that's headed up by a guy who was formerly a sex addict himself.

You're gifted. If you are looking for a place to use your gifts and help someone else, you should find more than enough oppportunities in the context of the *church.* Next time you go to church, look around the room and know that someone is walking in with a problem and that you have the answer for them. What a shame for you to walk out not having shared it.

The Healthy Church

You carry with you your faith, your unique needs, your unique hopes and expectations, and your unique gifts and talents every time you walk through the door of the church. Countless Spirit-filled people are out there with their needs, hopes, and expectations, just like you. Each one of us needs to use our gifts and talents to further the kingdom of God.

> There are diversities of gifts, but the same Spirit. There are differences of ministries, but the same Lord. And there are diversities of activities, but it is the same God who works all in all. But the manifestation of the Spirit is given to each one for the profit of all. (1 Cor. 12:4–7)

A healthy church operates with supernatural abilities and responsibilities. Paul says,

> For as we have many members in one body, but all the members do not have the same function, so we, being many, are one body in Christ, and individually members of one another. Having then [spiritual] gifts differing according to the grace that is given to us, let us use them. (Rom. 12:4–6)

The Rock Church has a specific calling to reach out to every person and every street in our county of San Diego. We have over one hundred community outreach ministries and over five hundred small group fellowships. The small group fellowships, youth groups, camps, and schools are committed to building strong Christians. The Rock's volunteer-led outreach ministries range from helping people find jobs, to refurbishing houses, to cooking, to painting, and much more.

> A healthy church operates with supernatural abilities and responsibilities.

The individuality and uniqueness of a church, beginning with the pastoral staff and leaders, extends through the entire organization, the congregation, and all of its ministries.

At a senior pastors' conference I attended, several of us sat around a table and discussed how we prepared our Sunday sermons. No two of us prepared in the same way. One pastor wrote out his sermon word for word the week before. Another pastor had his secretary write out an outline a month in advance as he dictated it to her. Another took time the night before and wrote out his sermon. Personally, I work on it a little bit at a time weeks in advance and tweak it after each sermon throughout Sunday. Our individual methodology works for each of us. The uniqueness of each pastor's preparation for Sunday services speaks of the creativity of God and the uniqueness of each church.

Just like your one-of-a-kind nose, teeth, eyes, and ears make up a one-of-a-kind face, so a group of one-of-a-kind individuals make up a one-of-a-kind church! Each unique church is part of God's global mosaic expression of Himself.

When God looks at the earth, He desires to see a full array of His creativity working through the individual congregations all around the world. As the church deals with the various problems that people and communities face, each member plays a unique and necessary role. It's important for you to become part of a local church where your uniqueness fits with the uniqueness of the church, so that together we fulfill God's great and wonderful plan for the global church and His global representation to the world.

In order to be healthy and strong, the church needs you and the gifts and talents God has given you. He designed each of us— whether we preach or paint or bring soup to the sick—to be an expression of His creative heart and the unique personality of each church. We have a man in our church who is gifted in finances, and through his financial stewardship classes, he has helped countless people get out of debt. God's gifts and calling are irrevocable, and *every one is useful in His kingdom.*

Ideas Need People

One of the things about me that can drive my staff crazy is that I have a thousand ideas a day. I am an idea junkie. I've learned that even though I have a lot of ideas, until they're shared with others, they'll never be as good as they can be. My gazillion ideas for our church are never the best version of themselves without a team collaborating with me. It's in that setting that God's creativity is polished and magnified, because it takes several of us to bring the idea to maturity. God gives me ideas, but it's only when my staff comes on board with me that the ideas can become what God intended them to be.

People will often come up to me and say they have a good idea, and I'll ask them if it's their idea or God's idea. Their idea may be good, but God's ideas will always be great.

I had an idea for a sermon series about relationships. My thought was to call it "Oneness." As we do for every sermon series, I called a meeting with our creative team to share my concept, and I asked them to pray and think about it and bring back ideas for discussion. God took the original idea to a whole new level when the creativity of the team began to flow. The original concept I had was turned into a clearer expression of what God actually wanted to be communicated.

The team suggested a new name, "Wired for Love," and they developed a marketing campaign using robots. They developed ways to impact people in the sanctuary, online, through the arts, with video, television, drama, spoken word, and media. The only way this could have happened was if those gifted in song, videography, web design, graphics, lighting design, stage and set design, and many more areas developed and expressed their uniqueness in partnership with others in the church. Without them I would've simply had an idea with a fraction of the impact it eventually had on lives.

Imagine if the church encouraged *everyone* to use their unique gifts with the ultimate goal being the true reflection of who God is and what God wants to accomplish.

It is critically important to value the gift God has given you and be true to that uniqueness. Be careful not to allow culture, your friends, or your insecurity to force you into someone else's mold. If you do, you will never be happy and fulfilled. Your God image is alive and actively trying to express itself and will only be satisfied when it is used the way God designed it.

Big Boy

I walked out of my office one morning, and a guy I had never met was just getting off the elevator. He was about six foot four, at least 250 pounds, and he wore cut-off jeans and a sweatshirt. His body was all tatted up. We started talking. His name was John. We walked down the hall together, and he told me he was going to his first ministry meeting, and he was really nervous.

"Nervous? How come you're nervous?"

"Pastor Miles, you always encourage us to do something, so I figured I got to do something. I want to serve the Lord."

Since our church has over a hundred outreach ministries, I asked him, "What's the ministry you're joining?"

"The knitting ministry," he said.

(DUDE! Knitting!)

"Well, actually, I don't knit, I *crochet*," he said.

(Oh sure. Now that made a lot more sense.)

Here's this huge guy who looks like he could be an NFL tackle, and he's nervous about joining a ministry that makes blankets and hats for hospitalized children.

Curious, I asked him where he learned how to crochet.

"I was in the Hell's Angels for twelve years," he told me. "I learned to crochet in prison. I know it's the one thing I can do for the Lord."

Just then the lady who heads up the knitting ministry walked toward us, said a quick hi to me, then asked the former Hell's Angel, "Are you John?" She gave him a big grin and took his hand. I watched them go down the hall together.

About a year later I was sharing this story from the pulpit, and right in the middle of the story, John, who was sitting in the front row, stood up in front of 3,400 people, wearing shorts and a T-shirt, and raised his tattoo-covered arms in the air. Crocheting may not seem like a unique ability, but when you package that with his life, the ripple effect can push countless others out of their comfort zone to step up and stand out the way God designed them to. Imagine if John was worried about what others would think about him crocheting for Jesus!

> It is in the church that we should be empowered and instructed to uniquely express the gifts God has given us.

By the way, John walked up to me the other night in church and asked me what my favorite colors were because he wants to crochet something for me.

The church needs to give us the freedom to be the people God uniquely called and created us to be. It is in the church that we should be empowered and instructed to uniquely express the gifts God has given us. The ways to serve God are endless. Serve Him on your job, in your school, at home, on the street, everywhere you go. The Bible is also clear about helping those in your *church family*. When you see a brother or sister hurting, grieving, hungry, or needy, you are to help them first. We take care of our own. "Bear one another's burdens, and so fulfill the law of Christ" (Gal. 6:2).

The image of God that we are to reflect includes not only God's compassion, love, patience, but also His discipline. In other words, when God calls your brothers and sisters to encourage you, they'll be there for you. When God wants you challenged, they will be there too. A ministry will pop up, and you'll be asked to take part in it when you don't think you're capable. This will be your opportunity to prove that "with God all things are possible" (Matt. 19:26).

At other times, if we get off track with Jesus, we need a little (or big) push from a wise and loving hand to put us back in line. God will send one of those same brothers and sisters to help us get back on track. The Bible says that "faithful are the wounds of a friend, but the kisses of an enemy are deceitful" (Prov. 27:6). It's a *faithful* brother who reaches out to you to remind you of God's purpose in your life. It's the *unfaithful* brother who tells you what you want to hear instead of what you need to hear when you're in spiritual need.

If you're going to realize the full potential of your calling and uniqueness, you'll need to live in union with a community of believers who are also committed to living consistent with God's image. A cell in the body can't do its job unless it works alongside other cells. This is one reason it is critical not only to attend church but also be connected with the people in the church. We need one another. "And let us consider one another in order to stir up love and good works, not forsaking the assembling of ourselves together, as is the manner of some, but exhorting one another, and so much the more as you see the Day approaching" (Heb. 10:24–25).

A Challenge for Church Knickknacks

My wife has decorated our house with little ornaments, dolls, plates, and figurines. I said to her, "Deb, what are these things around the house?" She said, "They're knickknacks. Some of them are works of art, but most are just knickknacks." They're just little cute things she puts around the house.

"So basically," I said, "what you're saying is that they are cute, they sit around, and they do nothing?"

"That's right," she said.

Are you a church knickknack—you get dressed up every Sunday and sit in your seat, and you do nothing?

James 1:22 says, "Be doers of the word, and not hearers only, deceiving yourselves." James 2:20 says, "Faith without works is dead."

Here's my three-part challenge:

One   Identify one place in your life where you've been out of sync with God. How have you been knick-knacking?

Two   Commit today to do what God tells you.

Three   Go to a pastor at your church *this week* and say, "I want to stop knickknacking. I want to *do something*. Put me to work." Then get busy giving all that love in you to serving the Lord.

PART 2

I

MORAL MIRROR

A
G
E

God created us as His moral mirror, so that when He looks at us He can see His very own character and holiness reflected back to Him and to the world. Yet in our pride, we all too often want to live independent of His guidance by creating our own morality. But God has provided us His own Son who came to cleanse and restore us to be a holy people.

Chapters 5–8 will guide us through the process of understanding and restoring the "M" in our God IMAGE: our role as a moral mirror!

5

Moral Mirror

A Right and Wrong Reality

In 2003, John Geoghan, an aging Catholic priest serving time as a convicted child molester and accused of molesting as many as 150 boys, was strangled to death in his prison cell by an inmate. The district attorney for the county told reporters that the convict who killed Father Geoghan considered the act a prize. The killer gained respect from the other prisoners for the murder and was regarded by some as a hero.

It's called *jailhouse justice* when convicts deal out their own brand of punishment on pedophiles and informants. Serial killer Jeffrey Dahmer was beaten to death in jail by an inmate. Jesse Anderson, incarcerated for stabbing his wife twenty-three times, was bludgeoned to death by the same inmate who killed Dahmer.

Jailhouse justice.

All societies have a code of ethics to follow, a system of what is considered right and wrong. Even in our prisons there exists a social hierarchy among prisoners based solely on their offenses. Certain crimes are more acceptable, while others are worthy of serious punishment by the inmates themselves.

I'm not a fan of jailhouse justice, but it does raise a question: Why does it exist?

The concept of right and wrong, no matter the basis, is an integral part of human society—from monasteries to street gangs to organized crime to the world of sports to the political arena to family life to job ethics. We would be hard-pressed to name a single activity that doesn't include a moral standard. Why?

Because the rule of right and wrong is rooted in all of us, and it comes from God. An atheist once told me, "Sometimes we just know something is right or wrong." Even though he denied the existence of God, he couldn't deny the existence of morality and the responsibility to exercise it. The Scriptures teach us that we are a "moral mirror" in the sense that God's sense of rightness, of justice, is firmly a part of who we are as humans.

As moral mirrors we don't have any holiness of our own; we have to rely on God to provide His holiness for our moral mirror to reflect. Our ability and responsibility to act as God's moral mirror is an aspect of being created in God's image.

God's Moral Standard

After church one day a guy asked, "If God can do everything, can He make a rock so heavy He can't pick it up?" Instead of giving him the yes or no answer he was setting me up for, I said, "God *can't* do everything."

He stepped back and frowned. "But I thought God, being God, can do everything."

"No," I repeated. "God can't lie. He can't deny His own holiness and perfect character."

God's holy character acts as a self-imposed boundary for Himself, and His morality limits His activities because He can't do anything dishonest or unjust. He's the undisputed heavyweight champion of rightness, the only Universal Lawgiver. He's Absolute Goodness. He's Absolute Justice. As our Moral Lawgiver, He is also Absolute Holiness. God *Himself* is the standard of right and wrong and moral perfection.

> God Himself is the standard of right and wrong and moral perfection.

Numbers 23:19 informs us that "God is not a man, that He should lie." Titus 1:2 and Hebrews 6:18 repeat this immutable fact: *it is impossible for God to lie.* Isaiah 45:19 says God is righteous. *Righteous* means a state of rightness that always does what ought to be done. If that is the case, a perfect moral character is the only thing that God can possibly project onto us, like light is projected onto us from a flashlight.

If He is projecting His holy character onto us as moral mirrors, what do you think He expects to see when He looks at us?

Answer: Holiness!

Being a moral mirror is not about your figuring out how to imitate God as much as you reflecting who God is back to Him and to the world.

Man's Moral Standard

I was so excited when my wife got pregnant with our first child, because I was so ready to be a dad and I wanted a girl. So when our first child was born, and it was a girl, I fell big time in love all over again. But this love was different. As soon as she came out, I was trying to figure out how I could get one of the robes the nuns wore at my Catholic school growing up. I figured she could wear that until she got engaged.

You might be thinking, there would be no engagement if she wore that. Exactly! I didn't want people holding her, getting perfume on her, sneezing on her. She was our princess, and I wanted to keep her all to myself so that nothing would spoil her baby smell, get her sick, or ruin what, to us, was perfection.

We as parents long to see our children find their purpose in life without taking painful and dead-end detours. Even more so, the Father desires to see His over-the-top purposes fulfilled in us.

Holy means to be set aside for God's divine purpose. This does *not* mean we should spend all our time in holy places, like church or Bible studies, as important as these places are. God just wants us to Himself for His purposes. He does not want to share you with anyone. He wants and deserves to be the focus of your life and thoughts.

I used to think the holy water in Catholic churches was H_2O plus some Holy Ghost swirling around in it. When I was a kid in Catholic school, I thought that if I drank it, I might start glowing or something. In reality, holy water is H_2O "set aside for a specific (and holy) purpose."

We have also been set aside. God spoke to the Israelites in Leviticus 11:45: "You shall therefore be holy, for I AM holy." We read these words, and we realize that He expects us to be holy like *Him*. We were designed to be His moral mirror, reflecting His perfect moral character back to Himself and to the world. God designed us to love as He loves, forgive as He forgives, show patience as He is patient, be encouraging as He encourages, administer justice as He is just, and uphold that which is right and good, as He does what is righteous and good.

Moral Integrity

If I were to show you an apple sitting in a bowl and ask you what it was, you would say it was an apple. If you cut it open, you would recognize it as an apple on the inside too. If I were to show you a banana, the same thing would happen. From the outside you can see it's a banana. You peel it, and it's a banana inside too. Then you look at someone who claims to believe in God. They look like a believer, they may say things that sound like a believer, but if you were able to look on the inside, what would you see? Integrity means being the same on the inside as on the outside. Our daily life—attitude, behavior, and thoughts—should match our prayer life.

We know that we are standing before God when we're in prayer, but the fact is, we're always standing before God. Next time you pray, listen to yourself and compare it to your conversation with others or to the self-talk in your head. As moral mirrors, we were created to think God's thoughts as well as speak God's words. We were intended to display the same moral integrity on the inside as well as on the outside.

Moral Reality

Not only did God create you as a moral mirror, to be a person of integrity, but He designed you with safeguards to remind you when you choose to stray. In the end, it's your choice to live with integrity, according to your original design.

One Sunday I asked the congregation of people to say Amen if they knew an area of their life that does not please God. The room shook with Amens.

Then I asked how many knew how to fix it. The room shook with Amens again.

Then I asked how many were willing to fix it today. Crickets. Very few said Amen. You know what you are doing wrong. God has revealed it to you, and if you ignore it, why blame God for the consequences?

Moral Absolutes

I was in a debate with a guy about whether or not Jesus was the only way to heaven. He thought there were many ways to heaven and accused me of being intolerant.

I responded with, "If *you're* truly tolerant, you need to tolerate my belief that you're wrong. If you refuse to accept my belief that you're wrong, then you're intolerant."

He said, "Huh?"

"Besides," I continued, "being tolerant, as you define it, is not my belief. I believe that there is an Absolute Truth." ("Tolerant" is often defined as giving people the right to believe what they want to believe, and to believe that every truth is equally true.)

Some things are simply right and some things are simply wrong—all the time, everywhere. When I said I believe in Absolute Truth, my opponent said there are no absolute laws of right and wrong, and that all truth is relative. I asked him if he was sure that there were no absolute right or wrong laws, and he said he was sure. I said, "Absolutely sure?"

He said, "Yes, absolutely!"

I asked, "Isn't that an absolute statement?"

Silence.

There are particular universal truths that I think all of us would agree are true. Rape, for example, is always wrong. Child molestation is *always* wrong.

You may live in a society where people believe moral absolutes don't exist, and you might ask one of these well-meaning people, as I do, "If there are no moral absolutes, are you saying rape is not wrong all the time?"

"Oh that's different," comes the quick response. "Of course rape is wrong all the time."

"And murder?"

"Yes, murder is wrong."

You continue: "And what about child abuse? Is pedophilia not wrong?"

"Of course it's wrong!" They will even get disgusted and offended when you ask if child molestation is absolutely wrong! They have no idea how they are contradicting their own claims of relevant truth.

When we look at the truth of human morality, there *are* moral absolutes. Morality must have an *absolute*. Morality must have a *basis*.

People fight for justice every day in the courts of the world. Societies long for law and order, because only then can a semblance of peace among people be maintained.

Without absolutes, morality is meaningless; who's to say what's right and wrong? Who's to say what's just and unjust? Is there any evidence that can distinguish right from wrong?

Moral Evidence, a Matter of Life and Death?

When you think of great women in history, Mother Teresa may come to mind. She dedicated her life to providing the best quality of life to the dying and poorest of the poor on the streets of Calcutta. Everyone would agree she was a good person. On the other hand, when you consider a madman like Adolf Hitler, a self-proclaimed killing machine, responsible for the deaths of over six million innocent people, you have to consider him an evil man.

But who is to say one was right and the other wrong? What makes Mother Teresa good and Hitler bad?

It's a matter of life and death. Let me put it this way: Suppose you're given a brand-new Mercedes and the dealer tells you to put high-octane gas in the tank. You decide you want to put water and sand in the tank. You think, "Who is the dealer to tell me what to put in the tank?" This decision about what to pour into the tank will determine the life or death of the engine. If you take care of your engine and keep the right gas in the tank, it will run well. If you put water and sand in the tank of that new Mercedes, you won't be going anywhere.

God's morality is based on rules and guidelines that fit the function of what He created. When we use or treat something in a way that is inconsistent with its function, it breaks apart or dies. When we use something according to what it was designed for, it functions well and lasts as long as it was intended to last.

If there's no absolute moral standard, then no one has a basis for determining good and evil. Mother Teresa and Adolf Hitler would just be two people doing what they felt like doing. Do you see how ludicrous that is?

Our Moral Mirror's Frame

God has given us clear parameters to His morality, a frame for our moral mirror. It is God's Word. Psalm 119:9 says, "How can a young man keep his way pure? By guarding it according to your word" (ESV). Just as God's holiness acts as a boundary around His actions, His Word acts as a limit to your morality. He is telling you, "As long as you keep yourself within the boundaries of My Word, My written Word, My spoken Word, My whispered Word, you'll be blessed."

Living consistent with God's Word means simply obeying His Word. Living in opposition to God's Word means living according to our own made-up set of rules. Do you know what that's called? It's called sin, and it leads to death (death of peace, death of joy, death of health, death of goodness, and finally, death itself). You've heard it said that we reap what we sow, and it's true. If we sow obedience to God and His Word, we'll reap the abundant, rich life that comes with it.

Take a sincere look at your life and see if you can identify a common theme that occurred whenever you acted outside of God's Word. Eventually something in your life probably died, such as a relationship, a career opportunity, or financial freedom. As a moral mirror, our responsibility is to live inside the parameters of God's Word, and then and only then will we reflect the moral character of God Himself.

6

Morality Maker

God Made in My Image

I sat next to a woman I'd never met before at a dinner party, and wouldn't you know, we started talking about God. (I wonder how that happened?) She began explaining her beliefs that God lives in all of us and we're all little gods. I listened patiently, nodding my head, as she went on that we're masters of our own lives and evil is just an illusion. "We need to become one with ourselves and the universe! We need to be at peace within and without," she said with her hands in prayer position. She continued at length about treating people as they want to be treated, and that we all have an inner light that we should tap into.

"Hmm, that sounds interesting," I said. "I agree that all human beings are precious, of course, but let me ask you a question. If I want to research and study about your faith's belief system, where would I find the information?"

She began repeating most of what she'd already said, and I asked her again, "If I want to learn about your beliefs, where would I find the information? Is there a single well-documented source? A book or something that contains or outlines your beliefs?"

She stuttered a little, then said, "Well, you can look inside of yourself."

"But what if I claimed to find something inside of myself different from and contradictory to what you claim to find inside of yourself? Who will be right?"

She said, "You can also look to the *universe* for answers."

"Okay," I said, "if I were to read up on the universe, as you say, where would I go? Do I call NASA? Do I study astronomy?"

Her hands fell to her sides. She gave me that look.

A silent pause passed between us and I said, "You just made all that stuff up, didn't you?"

When God created us as moral mirrors, He gave us the ability and desire to reflect and represent His moral character, not our own. Because our God image actively wants to administer justice in the world, we become an I AM imposter when we decide we don't need God, and our desire to reflect God's morality is turned into a desire to create our own morality. That's when we turn our back on fulfilling our God-given role as a moral mirror and begin pursuing the role as a *morality maker*.

Moral Responsibility

When I was a youth pastor, I took a group of young people to bring shoes, clothes, and food to people in Tijuana, Mexico. Our kids loved serving the orphanage, and I loved seeing our kids take the lead to serve. As I was standing outside the church, a barefoot little girl in a dress walked up the hill and extended her hands to me and said with her little voice, *"Necessito zapatos. Por favor. Zapatos."* I need shoes, please.

I thought, "We have plenty of shoes." But God spoke to me in a small voice and said, No zapatos. He said not to give her any shoes. Why wouldn't God want me to give this girl shoes? But as His moral mirror, my job was to simply obey, whether I understood or not. So I looked down at her and said, "No *zapatos*."

She wandered off, and eventually one of the teenagers in the group handed her some shoes. A minute later, the pastor came out of the church and told me not to give the girl any shoes because she wasn't poor and didn't need shoes. Her mother had become her daughter's morality maker, sending her over to act poor and then bringing the shoes to her to sell to the poor people in the village. It was a scam.

As God's moral mirrors, we are to *obey God*. But morality makers, on the other hand, make up their own rules for right and wrong. Our responsibility before God is not to make our own rules but to obey *His* rules. He wants us to listen for His voice rather than do what our own twisted logic is telling us.

Satan's Weapon, Part Two: Becoming a Morality Maker

In Genesis 3, Satan influences Adam and Eve to believe they don't need God and could be like God by knowing good and evil on their own. They could decide, without God's input, what's right and what's wrong. They could make up their own rules. This is what I AM imposters get in their heads, and it starts with the elimination of moral boundaries. I AM imposters don't pray "Thy will be done" but "*my* will be done," and this is part two of Satan's biggest weapon. It's the lie that you can decide for yourself what's right and wrong and suffer no consequences for your actions. Satan convinced Adam and Eve that they would "surely not die" for disobeying God. Satan is, as the Bible declares, "a murderer from the beginning" and the father of lies (John 8:44), and of course, Adam and Eve suffered the worst kind of death: being expelled from the presence of God.

Satan will ask you why you listen to God telling you right from wrong when you can figure it out on your own. Satan will always try to persuade you to believe that right and wrong are a matter of discretion, situational ethics, or personal preference. His goal is to remove all of God's moral boundaries from humanity.

Imagine the chaos. Imagine the cruelty and suffering.

Broken Boundaries

God put a frame around us as the moral mirror of His image. This frame is the *Word of God*. God's Word defines His morality, and we're born to reflect that image. A morality maker, on the other hand, ignores the Word of God, breaks God's frame, redefining the parameters of right and wrong, replacing it with what makes him or her feel good or what offers the most acceptance from others.

God's moral guidelines never change; they're timeless, the same yesterday, today, and tomorrow, and forever (Heb. 13:8). His Word never fades away or is canceled. The Lord's Word endures forever (1 Peter 1:25). God's loving, safe boundaries are eternally dependable and relevant. But knowing that this frame exists is not good enough; we must place our faith in it and obey.

Good Spirit, Bad Spirit

I recently spoke at a conference for organizations that help kids get out of gangs. After I briefly introduced myself, I explained to the crowd that even though I was there representing the faith-based community, every organization in the room, including those who represented the government, is a faith-based organization. Some have faith in education; others, money; some, tolerance; and others believe in government intervention.

Even street gangs are faith-based organizations. Some of them put their faith in violence, drugs, prostitution, and money. Every morality maker is a faith-based spiritual person, just like the woman I told you about at the beginning of this chapter who believes in the "universe." The questions are, what spirits are influencing them, and how can we recognize a good spirit from a bad spirit? Is it possible to be spiritually *wrong*?

Since we are spiritual beings, we can't underestimate both the good and bad spiritual influences in our lives. Demon spirits are the fallen angels who follow Satan. They're full of hate like Satan, and they connive to hinder and eliminate the good that God brings into the world and our lives. The I AM imposter I've been talking about is influenced by these bad spirits, instigating independence from God. The morality maker, without realizing it, acts as a mirror of Satan's character. When God looks at the morality maker, instead of seeing Himself reflected back, He sees a blurred image at best, if not complete darkness.

> Since we are spiritual beings, we can't underestimate both the good and bad spiritual influences in our lives.

Demons have personalities. Demons have the ability to think, reason, and live in relationships. Demons can communicate with us and deceive us. The Bible says that Satan can transform himself into "an angel of light" (2 Cor. 11:14).

You and I are spiritual beings with bodies designed to be spiritually guided and empowered by *God*. If we're influenced by *bad spirits*, our lives will be guided and influenced in an ungodly and distorted way.

Your God image never remains static in you, and once you're separated from Him, your God image will actually turn *against* God. Being willfully opposed to living as He's ordained you to live is the same as being willing to live consistent with Satan's advice and direction.

How can you tell if a bad spirit or God's Holy Spirit is leading you? Look at the evidence. God's Holy Spirit never lies, and He always, always, *always* encourages us to live in a way that's consistent with God's heart. Jesus told the disciples, "When He, the Spirit of truth, has come, He will guide you into all truth" (John 16:13) and "It is the [Holy] Spirit who gives life; the flesh profits nothing. The words that I speak to you are spirit, and they are life" (John 6:63). Remember, God can't contradict Himself. His Holy Spirit will always reinforce His holy character, which will always be consistent with His Word. The Bible tells us to test the spirits: "Beloved, do not believe every spirit, but test the spirits, whether they are of God; because many false prophets have gone out into the world" (1 John 4:1).

Deceived?

Morality makers are led by evil spirits who cause separation from God. Separation from God leads to spiritual death, which is far worse than physical death. The Bible warns us, "Be sober, be vigilant; because your adversary the devil walks about like a roaring lion, seeking whom he may devour" (1 Peter 5:8).

A person separated from dependence on God is still active with a drive to be creative, to express freedom, to think, and to reason. The problem is that the direction is contrary to *God's* direction.

I AM imposters become morality makers who are all about self and not about God. There are severe consequences for separating ourselves from God in this way. We think we can choose what's right for us; we think we can fill our heads and hearts with resentment and do whatever feels good, whether God approves or not. When we create a fertile environment for crime, murder, rape, robbery, and loss of integrity on all levels; when we're into deceit, lust, and greed; when we approve relationships that are about taking and not giving; when we live to selfishly benefit ourselves and not others; when we pursue goals to glorify ourselves and not God, we've chosen a lifestyle that will ultimately crash and self-destruct.

Remind yourself of John 10:10: The thief comes to steal, kill, and destroy, but Jesus has come so you can have life, and have it more abundantly.

Cocaine

During my rookie year with the San Diego Chargers, some of my teammates brought me into a hotel room to meet with a few of our other teammates. I was new to the team and trying to learn names and develop relationships. While hanging out in the room, one of the players pulled out some cocaine and put it on a table.

I'd never done cocaine and was somewhat scared of it, but my friend subtly nodded that it was cool. So I snorted a little powder that day, and it was the first day of about two years of using cocaine. I didn't realize that was also the first day I'd begin to reprogram my brain chemistry to actually *desire* cocaine. I didn't realize that I was training my brain to crave something that would destroy my body and everything I had worked for all my life.

Morality makers don't realize that any choice against the Lord's plan is self-destructive. Proverbs 21:30 says that no wisdom or understanding or counsel can stand against the Lord. The Bible says there's a way that seems right to a man, but in the end it leads to death (Prov. 14:12). Once you begin thinking you can change the rules, you'll find yourself addicted to death.

You might have heard the verse that says, "If God is for us, who can be against us?" (Rom. 8:31).

But the opposite is true as well. If God is against you or you are against God, who can be for you? You cannot defy God and think that there will be no consequences. That's Common Sense 101.

I was convinced that doing drugs was okay for me. I even thought it was *good* for me. I felt like I had a new identity. It didn't take long for my body to *crave* the cocaine and the feeling it gave me, and one year led to two, until I had messed up my brain so much that I was addicted to death. As a morality maker, I believed right was wrong and wrong was right.

"Religious" Morality Makers

There are morality makers in church too! In John 8, when the religious Pharisees caught a woman in adultery, they brought her to Jesus in an attempt to catch Him contradicting some point of religious law. They asked Him what to do with the woman: Should they stone her to death as the law prescribed? In the process, they exposed the classic characteristics of religious morality makers. They hijacked the *relationship-based* purpose of God. God is not about religious rules; He's about love and personal relationship.

It's possible to impose a set of religious rules on God's people that drains all the love out of faith. In the New Testament, the Pharisees were so manically glued to the Law of Moses that they couldn't recognize Jesus, who was the fulfillment of the law.

Religious legalism is like a drug that can suck the love out of our God relationship. Our connection and devotion to God should be completely based on our love for Him. Morality makers *need* to have rules in order to feel they're *doing* what's right. They can justify cruel, judgmental behavior with their harsh rules. Because these rules are like a drug, the morality maker *needs* to impose them on others in order to feel in control and to feel that he or she is better than others.

Jesus showed the accused woman love and compassion, allowing her to repent and be forgiven. The Bible tells us "God is love" (1 John 4), and all He does is love centered. Morality makers create a religious system that seeks and serves a god who resembles themselves. They worship a god who honors their own good intentions and reinforces *their* concepts of right and wrong.

Once the devil has established an I AM imposter identity in us and has us believing that we're our own god and that we can decide right and wrong for ourselves with no bad consequences for our actions, our lives will be about constantly trying to validate our identity. We can't stop. This is what Satan tried to use against Jesus in Matthew 4. Jesus is out in the wilderness after having just fasted forty days and nights, and the devil shows up and taunts Him. The devil challenges Jesus to *prove* Himself and validate His identity as God's Son. Jesus combats his taunts with the simple words, "It is written . . ." Jesus knew the Bible, He knew His Source, and He knew Himself.

Almost Good

There's a car wash near my house with one of those fun-house mirrors outside. If I stand in front of it one way, my head is elongated like a tree with two eyes. Another way, and my legs become chubby stumps and my stomach swells out like a lightbulb. Whenever I move, the shape of my body changes into something weird. But every now and then, if I move into just the right position, I'll get a clear and accurate image of myself. Because we're all made in the image of God—an image that was intended to do good things—we can show compassion, be generous, act with kindness, and show thoughtfulness. But like looking in a fun-house mirror, it is not the good God intended for His image to do. People who don't walk with God, though created in God's image, have redefined the definition of good. Even though God made them in His image, they have in turn made God and His goodness in their image. Every now and then you think you see an appearance of the pure image of God, but it's only an illusion.

When God looks at you every day, He expects to see His heart and His glory reflecting from your life. Instead of the distorted, blurred mirror, He wants to see *the real you* reflecting His heart and mind. God expects not just a glimpse of Himself in your outward appearance, but He wants a clear picture of Himself in a heart totally surrendered to Him.

The homeless derelict we saw at the beginning of chapter 2 wasn't always sleeping in alleys and scavenging in trash. The Mercedes-driving businessperson and soccer mom didn't always think they were God's gift to the world. Somewhere along the way they gradually bought into the lies the devil was feeding them. They thought they could decide right and wrong on their own and suffer no consequences, but gradually the death that God promised will result from sin.

Your body and soul crave to live joyfully and freely, but you can keep forcing it to live contrary to its design. Before long, you grow accustomed to being disappointed, failing, settling for second best, being let down, being used, being unappreciated. You become numbed to cursing, lying, and cheating, and you figure that's just how it is.

Hate wears you out. Jealousy wears you out. Failure is exhausting. Gossip tears you down. Stress makes you old before your time. Pride destroys you.

God has a better life for you! Obey God and surrender to Him. Obedience to Him isn't a noose around the neck, it's a key to truly being set free.

7

Light of the World

Human Light

There are three times in a woman's life when she seems to *glow*. When a woman falls in love, there seems to be something physically beaming out of her face. Then she glows at her wedding. At first I thought it was the white dress, but no, it is the glow of a bride. Then there's the glow of a pregnant woman. There's just something fresh and bright about a woman's countenance at these times, at least in my humble opinion.

The naked eye can't see any actual light shining out of the woman's skin, but biophotonics reveal that the human body *does*, in fact, emit light. The intensity of the light emitted by the body is a thousand times lower than the sensitivity of our naked eyes and could be due to changes in our metabolism. Scientists have proven that the human body directly and rhythmically emits light in extremely small quantities at levels that rise and fall during the day.

There's a correlation between being healthy and producing more light. The light we emit is produced because of the rapid multiplication of cells, and the faster the cells multiply, the more light one gives off. Children have cells that reproduce faster than they die, which produces more light, but older people's cells die faster than they reproduce, so less light is given off. If we give off more physical light when we're *physically* healthy, imagine the spiritual light that we give off when we are *spiritually* healthy.

In this chapter we'll focus on how Jesus saves us from the spiritual death of being morality makers by restoring our status as moral mirrors, bearers of God's image designed to reflect God's moral character.

Jesus's Light

Jesus said in John 8:12, "I am the light of the world. He who follows Me shall not walk in darkness, but have the light of life." He is referring to the *spiritual* light that His righteousness provides to the world and to those who place their trust in Him.

Light is obviously useful for seeing in the dark, but as reflectors of God's image, we've been designed to emanate a *spiritual* light. This spiritual light isn't something we can concoct on our own, but it's the light that comes from our "hand in glove" relationship with the Light of the World.

Jesus wants us to be "the *light* of the world," "*a city . . . set on a hill* [that] cannot be hidden" (Matt. 5:14) because "God is light and in Him is no darkness at all" (1 John 1:5).

Our spiritual light doesn't come from us; it is the supernatural spiritual light from Christ Himself that shines through us. The Bible calls *you* the light of the world, because the presence of God in you is a light that gives guidance to a spiritually dead and dark world. "For you were once darkness, but now you are light in the Lord. Walk as children of light" (Eph. 5:8).

WWJD

A few years back there was a slogan you'd see everywhere on hats and bracelets and T-shirts: WWJD. It stood for "What Would Jesus Do?" It's a good thought, but the true spiritual way of living out the WWJD slogan would be to change it to WWJDTM, "What Would Jesus Do *Through Me?*"

We were created in His image so He could fit perfectly inside of us and express Himself perfectly through us. The only way we can do what Jesus does is by being filled with His Spirit, obeying His Word, and surrendering to His leading.

Have you found yourself trying to figure out what Jesus would do and then trying to do it yourself in your own strength in your own way? Why don't you ask Jesus what He wants to do and then let Him do it through you Himself? When Christ starts living through you, the Father will see Himself in you as though He is looking in a mirror.

> Our spiritual light doesn't come from us; it is the supernatural spiritual light from Christ Himself that shines through us.

We can try to copy the patience and kindness Jesus had when He was on the earth, but we have to remember that His patience and kindness, His miracles and acts of compassion were the result of His complete surrender to the Father. "I do nothing on my own but speak just what the Father has taught me" (John 8:28 NIV).

Make a careful study of the life of Jesus. Study His words, His actions, His works, His miracles. You'll see that He was one with His heavenly Father and lived His life submitted to Him. It was the Father who empowered and anointed Him with the Holy Spirit during His life on earth. Jesus's every thought and deed was surrendered to God.

WWJD, What Would Jesus Do?, can also be What Would Jesus *Desire*? Or WWJF, *Feel*? Or WWJT, *Think*? After all, it's Jesus who now fits in us like a hand in a glove, living His life through us. Remember, a glove doesn't move on its own, it's moved by the hand that's inside it. Galatians 2:20 says, "I have been crucified with Christ; it is no longer I who live, but Christ lives in me; and the life which I now live in the flesh I live by faith in the Son of God, who loved me and gave Himself for me."

Because of that perfect fit, the spiritual light that you're designed to reflect comes from the Holy Spirit in your heart. It's Christ's righteousness that we have, not our own. Paul says in Philippians 3:9, "And be found in him, not having a righteousness of my own that comes from the law, but that which comes through faith in Christ, the righteousness from God that depends on faith" (ESV).

Who can reflect the moral perfection of God better than God Himself?

Heart Vision

We can't fool God with a righteousness of our own, because God looks at the heart and sees our intentions, our thoughts, and our desires. When Christ has complete control of our hearts, He has control of our lives, and only then can our lives become mirrors of God's moral character.

During a job interview in the early years of our church, a candidate made a comment that he heard I was a difficult person to work for because I want everything done NOW. He said he heard that I wasn't patient about letting the process run its course.

I explained to him that what's more important to me than the completion of the project is knowing that the project is making progress. I would like evidence—not some subjective, nondescript feeling—that progress is being made. How many people were there compared to the last meeting? Were there testimonies of changed lives? Did someone serve, teach, or pray who has never done so before?

We can fool ourselves that we are living right. We can say that everything is "great" and never define what "great" is. We can say that we're making progress and yet avoid looking for proof that this is true. But we cannot fool God, who knows all things, including the thoughts and intents of our hearts.

> When Christ has complete control of our hearts, He has control of our lives, and only then can our lives become mirrors of God's moral character.

God is not just as concerned about our being perfect as He is about the desire in our hearts to honestly pursue perfection and holiness. He sees the evidence in the fruit of our lives. He is the righteousness that we need to be transformed into.

He wants and expects to see progress in our lives. He wants to see an increasing level of surrender to the desires of Christ in our decisions and attitudes.

Colossians 3:9–10 says, "Do not lie to one another, since you have put off the old man with his deeds, and have put on the new man who is renewed in knowledge according to the image of Him who created him." We can't sit around and assume that just because Jesus is in our life, He'll cover everything we do with His holiness, thus leaving us irresponsible. We need to be renewed into the image of the God who lives in us. It's true that the Father sees Himself in us through His Son, but He's also looking at how much we're submitting to the Son and how much that submission is actually transforming our actions and attitudes into those of Jesus.

There are way too many commands directing us to act by faith for us to think we have no responsibility to be diligent about obeying. For instance, we're told to pray without ceasing (1 Thess. 5:17; 1 Tim. 2:8). We're told the way to speak that pleases God and what to think about (Phil. 4:8; Eph. 4:29). We're told we'll be blessed if we spiritually hunger and thirst for righteousness (Matt. 5:6).

We're told to bless our enemies, to give, to serve, to do all of the things Jesus did on earth. We need to allow Jesus to do these things through us. The more we voluntarily surrender to Christ's desires, the more of His presence and loving personality will be seen and experienced by those around us. Remember, to whom much is given, much is required, and we couldn't have been given more than the I AM Himself taking up residency inside of us.

Flashlights

Every summer our parents took us on vacation in upstate New York. In those pitch-black summer nights in the woods, we couldn't see two feet ahead of us. My sisters and brothers all shared one flashlight, so we would all hold hands and follow the person in the front with the light. Without that light, we couldn't see where we were going.

The purpose of God's light is to enable us to see the way God wants us to go, to show us how to live. When He shows us how to live, our life can show others how to live, because our lifestyle is consistent with God's moral standard.

But, you might ask, *how* does He show us His way to go? *How* does He guide us? The answer is, not only do you have the Holy Spirit within you, you have the light of the truth of *His Word*! "Your word is a lamp to my feet and a light to my path" (Ps. 119:105).

The Holy Spirit reveals to our hearts the truth found in God's Word, empowers us to live up to God's moral standard, instructs us and shows us our boundaries, and establishes in our hearts the frame to our moral mirror.

Jesus Is the Word

> In the beginning was the Word, and the Word was with God, and the Word was God. He was in the beginning with God. All things were made through Him, and without Him nothing was made that was made. In Him was life, and the life was the light of men. (John 1:1–4)

Jesus Christ *is* the Word. When we instill His words into our hearts, the Holy Spirit sets fire to our hearts and the words become alive in us. "'Is not My word like a fire?' says the LORD" (Jer. 23:29). It was a *word* spoken by God that brought the world into being. God is one with His Word. (See also Heb. 4:12.)

When you memorize and speak the Word of God aloud to yourself, you're memorizing and speaking God into your heart as well as into the hearts of others. "Man shall not live by bread alone; but man lives by every word that proceeds from the mouth of the LORD" (Deut. 8:3). Because the Word is living and active, it consistently interacts with and reestablishes the integrity of our moral mirror, and the more our moral mirror is polished, the more we can be lights to others.

Illuminating, Not Blinding

I was planning a sermon series in which I wanted to give the appearance of heaven in the sanctuary. We needed sound, earthquake-like shakes, beautiful music, and blinding light. I asked how bright of a light they could shine on the crowd, and my production team told me that they had blinders that would actually "white out" a room full of people. (I remembered being at a concert when they blasted those blinders in my face, and I did *not* like it.)

Blinding us isn't God's intent—He doesn't want to wipe us out with more truth than we can handle. His light reveals truth in a way that enables us to obey and be transformed by it. The act of restoring the potential and power of our moral mirror is a *process*. He doesn't reveal all of our wrongs to us at once, but gradually.

While approaching a stoplight, I drove past a fast-food restaurant where a lady was trying to exit. I was looking in her direction, somewhat daydreaming and not paying attention. I didn't realize she was asking to get out until I was already passing her, but it seemed to her that I looked right at her and intentionally cut in front of her. She made it clear with several different hand gestures that she was ticked off that I didn't let her out.

I felt really bad for about an hour. Even though I didn't see her in time, all I could think about was how selfish it must have looked. Can you imagine if God showed us *all* of our guilt at *one time*? I think we could become suicidal after seeing the extent of our ego, jealousy, pride, and self-centeredness.

Think about it this way: imagine if everything you thought in your mind came out as words exactly the way you initially thought them. That's like walking up to someone and saying exactly what you were thinking. See what I am saying? We have a lot of bad stuff in our hearts that God reveals to us little by little so as not to depress us but to allow us to surrender all of it to Him. God knows that the more right you do, the more right you want to do.

The light He shines in your heart is a very sensitive light that reveals the moral lessons that you can handle at the time. Consequently, when God calls you to be a light to others, He wants to see you gently and lovingly providing light for others so they can find their way, not the kind of light that hurts the heart and blinds the eyes.

One of the main reasons I turned my life over to Christ was because I watched two guys walk with God. The manner in which they conducted themselves revealed God's truth to me. One was loud and funny but respectful and respected. The other was quiet, humble, and respectful. Both were following Christ in a way that I knew I wanted to. They were different from each other, but both were moral mirrors. The example of their lives was a light to me, revealing how the truth of God's Word was to be lived out.

Feed the Dog

Imagine two Doberman pinschers living in your heart. One Doberman is a good dog, encouraging you to be strong, to obey God, and to read God's Word. This is the Holy Spirit, the good dog. The other Doberman is *not* good, and it fights for control of your life. (This is your morality maker in you wanting to do what *it* wants to do.) These two dogs fight every day for control of your life.

Ephesians 6:12 tells us clearly that we don't wrestle against flesh and blood but against the evil principalities and powers. Galatians 5:17 explains how those principalities and powers fight with us: "For the flesh lusts against the Spirit, and the Spirit against the flesh; and these are contrary to one another, so that you do not do the things that you wish." But as bearers of God's image, we understand John 3:6 telling us, "That which is born of the flesh is flesh, and that which is born of the Spirit is spirit."

The dog that wins the battle is going to be the dog that you feed. Matthew 26:41 says, "Watch and pray, lest you enter into temptation. The spirit indeed is willing, but the flesh is weak."

You feed the good dog by

- studying God's Word: "Your *word* I have hidden in my heart, that I might not sin against You" (Ps. 119:11).
- praying God's Word: "This is my comfort in my affliction, for Your word has given me life" (Ps. 119:50).
- hanging with God-fearing people: "Let us consider how we may spur one another on toward love and good deeds, not giving up meeting together, as some are in the habit of doing, but encouraging one another—and all the more as you see the Day approaching" (Heb. 10:24–25 NIV).
- listening to and meditating on Bible-based sermons, teachings, books, and other Christian materials: "Be diligent to present yourself approved to God, a worker who does not need to be ashamed, rightly dividing the word of truth" (2 Tim. 2:15).

Move the Furniture

Five years after we moved into our last home, my wife started asking to get the walls painted. I told her the walls were already painted white. But no, she wanted one wall some foo-foo version of mustard orange, she just had to have a blood-red color on another wall and some version of green on half of another wall. I was cool with white. I felt like I was going to be living inside of a salad. I finally gave in, like a good husband, and called the painters. Included in their bid was a cost for moving the furniture. I wasn't about to pay someone to move my furniture. What did he think I had kids for?

So the day before the painters came, we began moving the furniture, and while we were carrying the couch from one room to another, my son asked, "What happens if they don't show up? We did all this work for nothing." (I think he was just trying to get out of doing the work.) I told him we had to move the furniture in *faith*, believing that the painters were coming the next day. Hebrews 11:1 says, "Now faith is the substance of things hoped for, the evidence of things not seen." Once we have God's Word *in* us, and we obey His Word by faith, we can trust a blessing is coming.

Hebrews 11:6 says, "But without faith it is impossible to please Him, for he who comes to God must believe that He is, and that He is a rewarder of those who diligently seek Him." You can't obey God and mirror His righteous ways of life without faith.

Vows

I recently officiated a wedding, and like all weddings, the people were dressed up and happy. The groom was a man I've known since he was a teenager, and he was looking good in his tux, and the bride was glowing in her long white wedding gown. Part of the ceremony was the lighting of the unity candle, symbolizing how the two shall become one in the marriage. Then it came time to take their vows, which they said out loud for everyone to hear. What was interesting to me was that during the vows, everyone was smiling, and not one person said that it was too soon to make a commitment to so many rules. No one stood up and said, "It's early. You're just getting started. Go with the flow for a while and see if things work out. You may want to loosen things up after a few months of being together and see other people."

Wedding vows are designed to *protect* a marriage. The vows are reasonable guidelines for how to protect the couple's love for each other and provide boundaries for their love in the future. The vows spoken by this couple were their opportunity to make a public confession of their commitment to one another.

Jesus not only makes vows to us, but He *keeps* His vows to us by living in us and *empowering us to keep our vows to Him*. He actually lives them through us, "for it is God who works in you both to will and to do for His good pleasure" (Phil. 2:13).

He's able to make you a vow-keeping moral mirror.

8

Mirror Polish

Perfect Love

During my first year as a youth pastor, I was placed on parking lot duty. While I was walking around, keeping watch on the cars during the church service, I saw some guy placing flyers on the windshields. I didn't recognize him, and I knew that the church didn't place flyers on the cars, so I walked up to him and sure enough, he was from another church, and he was advertising a healing service. I said, "C'mon, man, you can't be doing that here," and I asked him to remove the flyers. This apparent Christian brother from another mother, supposedly doing God's work, began yelling at me, trying to justify why his informing our people about his healing service was more important than respecting our rules. I explained that if we let one person do it, we'd have to let everyone place ads on our cars.

By now his face was turning red, and he began trying to talk me into bending the rules for him. He quoted Scripture in an effort to justify his right to do what he wanted on our property. Because I did not have the desire, much less the authority, to make that call, I told him flat-out, "Brother, do NOT put your flyers on the cars, and you need to remove the flyers you already handed out." Then he wanted to start an argument about our beliefs, about how his church was more spiritual because they spoke in tongues. I said, "Dude, I don't care if you speak in Spanish, French, and Swahili at the same time, you need to get the flyers off the windshields of our cars."

Then, if you can believe it, the guy started cursing at me. (I thought to myself, I know that I am a young pastor, but I don't think the *Loving My Christian Brother Handbook* allows cursing.) I paused, looked him in the eye, and said, "Brother, where's the love?"

Silence.

I continued. "You're able to quote Scripture and argue doctrine, but you're missing the most important point of the faith. LOVE!"

Almost in a whisper, with his head down, he said, "But I have love."

Brother, your love needs some work. This guy thought he had the right to do anything he pleased in the name of the Lord, but he left out love. Sometimes Christians spend so much time trying to *be* right that they forget about trying to *do* right, which is to express God's love, His *perfect love.*

If there's one thing we have to learn, it's how to love and love perfectly.

In this chapter we'll focus on the best way the church can polish our moral mirrors by equipping us to express perfect love.

Deception

The ancient book *Art of War* by Sun Tzu is one of the oldest and most successful books on military strategy in the world. Written 2,000 years ago by a Chinese general, one of the simplest statements in *Art of War* is "All war is deception." Simply, Sun Tzu is saying that to win at war, we need to employ deception in our tactics, such as "Attack an indirect target to distract our enemy from the main target. When he is distracted protecting the indirect target, attack the main target." He said to make the enemy prepare on the *left* because then he will be weak on the *right*.

The devil has for centuries successfully used deception to distract the church from keeping the main thing the main thing. Satan uses this deception to distract us into fighting an information war, an economic war, a political war, or a denominational war. When we spend all of our time arguing instead of loving, the church becomes better known for what it is against than what it is for.

Because we're distracted with secondary issues, we lose our focus on preparing and developing the perfect love God has commissioned us to share with the world. He commanded us to feed the poor, heal the sick, and encourage wounded hearts and souls. We're given the sacred and awesome calling to *love* souls into the kingdom of God. Loving God first and then loving our neighbor are the two greatest commandments, which make these the most important things we are to do in life (Matt. 22:37–40).

> When we spend all of our time arguing instead of loving, the church becomes better known for what it is against than what it is for.

Think about the non-Christians you know. How well would they say that you love them? Would they say that you love them at all, or would they simply say they know you and there is nothing about you that is different from the nonbelievers they know? If we express the love of God the way we were designed to, there would be no mistaking believers for nonbelievers.

One young girl told me, "When I look at my Christian friends, I don't see any difference between their life and mine, so why should I go to church? Why should I obey a bunch of laws and have some preacher tell me what I should do? Why should I hand over my money when I'm just as happy as they are and I get to keep my money and do what I want to do?"

Our focus isn't following a list of propositional truths, dos and don'ts, as much as it is placing our trust in the person of Jesus, who is foremost and essentially known for His *love*. We don't need more information, we need more love, more *love training*. The people who experience you should experience the love of Jesus. Your life is the strongest sermon you'll ever preach.

Three Kinds of Love

I remember my first girlfriend in high school. I was in "mad love." I couldn't think about school or anything else but that girl. All I wanted was to be with her. I was happy all the time. It was almost like I was on drugs. This obsession was fueled by what is called *eros* love. Eros is where we get the word "erotic."

Eros love is a passionate, mad infatuation. When you are in eros love, your brain is washed with a pleasure hormone called dopamine. (Dopamine is what cocaine stimulates your brain to release to give you its high!) This passionate, erotic love for someone is all-consuming and very addictive. Eros love is focused on feeling good—what you *get* versus what you *give*.

Because eros love seriously clouds your judgment, eros love blinds you to anything that will potentially disrupt the pleasure you get from the relationship. Your friends can tell you that they saw your new main squeeze with someone else, but your eros-blinded heart won't let you believe it's possible.

Unfortunately, the dopamine wash of eros only lasts for a short time, and then the passionate, erotic, all-consuming love feelings level off and your feelings balance out. Because you're used to passion and the all-consuming emotional rush of eros love, this dip in your emotional high becomes a transitional point in your relationship. It might be during this time that you'll either feel like you're falling out of love or you'll wonder if the other person is really the one for you. Eros love gave you such a love high that now you may begin to lose interest and consider going back on the hunt for a new eros love experience. What's most likely happening is that you're transitioning into a more mature love, sometimes referred to as *philia* love.

This next step in the development of love is friendship love. It's a brotherly, virtuous love, and it includes loyalty to friends, family, and community. In ancient texts, *philia* denoted a general type of love used for love between family, between friends out of a shared activity, as well as friendship between lovers. In philia love, you're ready to admit that the other person isn't exactly perfect after all. Now you have to decide if the imperfect person is worth your love or not.

Philia love is all about *genuine caring* and acknowledges give-and-take on a deeper level. It's about friendship and the development of a *mutual* respect. You begin to recognize and think about the *mutual* benefits of the relationship. Philia love provides a stronger foundation to build your love relationship upon than eros love, which is all about feeling good.

Philia love has a more mature foundation and is a mature version of love.

But there is still a deeper love experience.

The third kind of love is perfected love, *agape* love. It's God's love. Greek scholar Dr. Kenneth Wuest has said that eros and philia love are "elevated, purified, and ennobled" by agape love. It's a love that is bigger than us; it's a divine unconditional and unselfish love. You have agape love when you're willing to love and sacrifice for someone else with no expected or required reward other than the sheer pleasure of loving them. You make a commitment and covenant to love, no matter what.

Covenant Love

A friend of mine was married to a woman who cheated on him for over three years with multiple partners. She moved out of the house, but he continued to be committed to the marriage. She traveled across the country, and he followed her, pursuing his love for her even though it looked impossible that she'd ever come back to him. Eventually his love and persistence won her heart, and through counseling and prayer their marriage was restored. A marriage that looked completely hopeless was rescued, and they're together and happily married today.

My friend had much more than eros love for his unfaithful wife. He was driven by God's agape love, a covenant love.

Eros love is love for pleasure's sake.
Philia love is love for friendship's sake.
Agape love is love for love's sake.

Take a moment and ask yourself if your love for the people in your life has matured and been perfected to the agape love level. If it hasn't, you are more likely to abandon a relationship once things get shaky or difficult.

Loving God

We can go on this same roller-coaster ride in our love relationship with God. When we surrender our lives to Jesus and come to know God for the first time, we're in an eros type of love with God. We're so excited about the relationship that we run out and buy new Bibles with more study notes than we'll ever use. We tell everyone who'll listen about what we're learning in the Bible. We can't stop talking about the Lord. Everything God does for us is so exciting, and life is simply wonderful.

God put terrific new friends in your life. You can't get enough of church, spending three or four nights a week there, in addition to church on Sunday. Best of all, you finally found some inner peace. People might even think you are in a cult and have been brainwashed because they have never seen you so happy and obsessed. The sense that the good feelings would never go away was reinforced by the myth that because you're a Christian you'll be this happy all the time, and God will protect you from any and all bad things happening to you. You were in a state of ecstasy—you were in eros with God.

Not all new believers get so excited, but speaking for myself, when I got hold of God and let Him get hold of me, I was fired up. It was the honeymoon of my faith life. I told everyone on my Chargers team about Jesus. I invited everyone I could to Bible study, and I prayed with anyone who'd pray with me. The honeymoon was terrific!

Then the first trial hit.

I had just won the starting job as the San Diego Chargers' free safety, and to say that I was excited about the first game of the season would be an understatement. I was on top of the world! God was blessing me! But then it happened: the first big test of my faith. Two days before our first game against the Minnesota Vikings, I twisted my knee in practice. I ignored it, but when the time came to get on the bus and then board the plane, I was limping and in pain. Why would God do this to me? Why would God set me up and then let me down? (That's what the devil wanted me to think.)

God was nurturing *trust* in my life.

When we got to Minnesota I could barely walk to my room, and I had to miss the practice the day before the game.

I sat in the hotel room with ice on my knee, praying, *God, why would You let this happen to me? What did I do? Have You left me?* When I'd had enough of feeling sorry for myself, I was finally able to tell Him, "Not my will, but Yours." Then something amazing happened. I went to sleep that night, and when I woke up, the knee was *fine.* I played the entire game!

Have you ever thought that God left you? God will not *ever* leave you. Where is He going to go? He is everywhere! Even if I hadn't been able to play the Vikings the next day, God hadn't left me. He doesn't leave us! He said, "I will never leave you nor forsake you" (Heb. 13:5). Remember that. He just moves us to a more mature love that's more faith-based.

God doesn't love us with eros love. He loves us with agape love, love that is bigger than we are, love that is divine and perfect, never failing, and permanent. First John 4:8 tells us that God is agape, and it's agape that the Holy Spirit pours into our hearts (Rom. 5:5).

A turning point in our relationship with God occurs when the emotional eros love we've had comes against a trial. We can mistakenly think God is punishing us, or we can think that God has left us. None of that is true! When trials come,

Satan wants you to blame God, or at least doubt Him, when in fact God is training you to trust Him.

Philippians 1:6 says, "He who began a good work in you will bring it to completion at the day of Jesus Christ" (ESV). That "good work" is perfecting love in your heart. First John 2:5–6 goes on to say, "But whoever keeps His word, truly the love of God is perfected in him. By this we know that we are in Him. He who says he abides in Him ought himself also to walk just as He walked." One way we can tell that our love is perfected in Jesus is when we're supernaturally able to maintain His joy and peace in every circumstance.

Philia love gives us a more functional and healthy balanced relationship with God. This is when we learn to apply His Word to the ups and downs of life. Our love still isn't perfected yet, but we're growing. We need more knowledge and experience in our relationship with God to lead us to the third and highest love: *agape* love, the most healthy and powerful love known to humankind.

> When trials come, Satan wants you to blame God, or at least doubt Him, when in fact God is training you to trust Him.

Agape love is sacrificial and totally selfless—love for the sake of love, not for self-benefit. It's a love bigger than feelings. God loved us before we loved Him, and when it was of no benefit to Him, when there was no love whatsoever being expressed back to Him. As a matter of fact, what He got was antagonism, betrayal, and rebellion. He loved us unconditionally anyway.

Agape love is the kind of love that took Jesus to the cross to be crucified. In His unspeakable agony, He held on to His agape love for the Father and for us.

Agape love is only possible to experience through the Holy Spirit. We can't manufacture such love. We might try to imitate it, but we'll always come up short. Agape love isn't stationary; it grows and expands in us.

In 1 John 2:5 and 4:19, we're told that our love is perfected as God lovingly walks us through hard times, teaching us to love Him for who He is and not for what we get from Him. He teaches us to love through a covenant we have made with Him, a covenant that isn't shaken by circumstances.

Love Training

During my sophomore year in high school I signed up to perform in the school's musical production of *Guys and Dolls*. I didn't have to audition, I just signed up. Of course I had no acting experience, and could I sing? No! I only wanted to hang out with the girls who were in the show. I landed a role with one line. I also had to sing, and as I said, singing is *not* one of my strengths. So in one of the big musical numbers, twelve of us guys were lined up at the front of the stage to do the number "Luck Be a Lady." I was the last guy to the far right. At rehearsal we were doing the number, and while we were in the middle of it, the director stopped us and said something was not right. He told the six guys to the left not to sing, and the six guys to the right, where I was standing, to take it from the top. Three lines in, he stopped us. He told the three guys in the middle not to sing, and directed the three of us on the far right to take it from the top.

He was getting really warm. Two lines in he pointed to me and said, "You, don't sing!" Eleven guys did the number, and I lip-synced for the whole production. I had to learn how to act, how to walk across the stage, how to dance, and how to look like I was singing.

Our everyday life is a *real-life* drama, and it's *in* the drama that we learn how to act. You don't audition for this show.

You're in it with or without a good voice. In real life, when things don't go well, we learn to trust God. We learn to be thankful even when we don't get what we want. We learn to conquer fear with prayer. We learn to bless others, and we learn to give God honor and glory. We learn to trust God in the darkest times of our lives. *It's in the context of real life that we learn how to love.*

How many times have you had something unexpected or unwanted happen to you and you thought that the God of faithfulness was being unfaithful? You might be going through a trial now and find yourself doubting God. Stop it. God can't be unfaithful. It is against His perfect character to be unfaithful.

Michelle, an employee of our church, was seven months pregnant with her second child. She and her husband had lost their first child during the pregnancy, and then when they were enjoying this new pregnancy and the hopes and dreams of a baby, she gave birth prematurely to a stillborn. The people of the church visited her every day in the hospital to share their love and to encourage her and her husband. This was a real witness to the nurses and doctors. They were impressed that our pastors and staff also came and brought food, sat with them, prayed with them, encouraged them, and showed them that they wouldn't go through this alone.

The biggest encouragement came from Michelle and her husband, Chris (who also worked at the church). They were never negative, never self-pitying, and never did they doubt God's love or accuse Him of being wrong. Michelle and Chris could have easily been bitter toward God, but what we saw in them was faith and courage. We saw that the Holy Spirit had been at work in their lives, and they were *trained* how to *trust God* through even the most difficult times. They sent a clear message that their love for God was unconditional. It's possible to suffer and love God at the same time.

We have to learn how to endure pain with grace and love by holding on to God through hard times. We need to be able to proclaim, "God is good *all* the time," even through our tears. This is the truest, purest example of being God's moral mirror.

> We have to learn how to endure pain with grace and love by holding on to God through hard times.

We need to learn how to love the people around us, how to live with grace and genuine respect for one another. The church community gives us that opportunity. It's within the body of Christ, united with one another, that we're able to practice obeying God in every situation. If we allow God to use every situation to nurture an obedient heart, a perfect love will grow in our hearts.

PART 3

AUTHORITY TO RULE

God created the planet Earth and then gave us the authority to care for it with the expectation that He would see His creation flourishing in the way it would were He caring for it. To a large degree, we failed and ruined much of His creation.

In chapters 9–12 we will learn to exercise our God-given authority—the "A" in our IMAGE—in a way that mirrors the heart of God.

9

Authority to Rule

Creating Environments Where You Can Flourish

When my wife became pregnant with our first child, we were really excited but also a little nervous. We wanted to create the perfect place for our baby to live and grow. We bought the crib, the stroller, and the changing table. We painted the walls of her room, bought new baby blankets, curtains, a baby mobile, and a mountain of disposable diapers. Then came the baby showers and the baby gifts, the playpen, the high chair, the bouncing swing, the baby bathtub, the car seat, the tiny clothes, and the stuffed animals.

Of course, we prayed. A lot. After she was born, every night we wrapped her in a clean blanket all the way up to her eyes. When kids come through the vaginal canal, their soft heads get squeezed into a point. Our daughter's head looked like Gumby's. Only the tip of her little coned head was sticking out of the top of the blanket. We'd hold her tiny body in our arms and pray for her. Our ultimate desire and goal was (and still is) that our child would be all that God created her to be. But how would this be accomplished? We couldn't force her to be what we wanted; that's not the way God works in our lives, and it isn't a good way for parents to work either. All our preparations for our daughter created an environment where she could flourish as God's child, God's image bearer.

This idea brings us to the third aspect of being created in God's image, which is the *authority* God has given us to exercise dominion over creation. Preparing for the arrival of a son or daughter is just one example of how we exercise the authority and responsibility God gave us to make, create, and protect environments that ensure that His originally intended purposes are fulfilled. God has granted you the authority *to create nurturing environments* so His purposes will be fulfilled in the lives of His image bearers and everything He has created.

The Responsibility of Authority

After God created the heavens and the earth, He created Adam and Eve and gave them very clear instructions: "Then God said, 'Let Us make man in Our image, according to Our likeness; let them have dominion over the fish of the sea, over the birds of the air, and over the cattle, over all the earth and over every creeping thing that creeps on the earth'" (Gen. 1:26). Genesis 2:15 says God put Adam in the Garden of Eden to "tend and keep it."

He said, in effect, "Listen, the environments I created sustain life and facilitate the fulfillment of my original intent for creation. I want you to preserve this ability to maintain life. I want you to make sure that everything has what it needs to live." This is what God says to us too. "I gave you the *authority* to *take care of what's Mine.*"

God has given us the ability to understand how things work together, how they were created and designed, and how to ensure they fulfill the purpose for which they were created. Often all we need to do to accomplish what He wants is to protect the systems He originally set up, whether in nature or in relationships.

Authority's Limits

It's one thing to know the nature of the authority we've been given, and another thing to understand the *limits* of our authority. God did not give us authority over people.

As a husband, I have no God-given right to *rule* over my wife. Some men make that mistake. They treat their wives like servants, ordering them around, trying to control their lives. That's not what God meant when He said, "Wives, submit to your own husbands, as to the Lord" (Eph. 5:22). Nobody *owns* anybody. I don't *own* my wife. We're partners, lovers, and parents together, and we honor and respect one another. We flourish as a married couple because we support each other's purpose in life. God gave me my wife to love and to cherish, and to help her become all God created her to be. If you're a husband, the authority you have in the home is to nurture an environment in which your wife and family can thrive and prosper. Your job is *not* to control and manipulate.

Besides, I promise you fellas, if you allow yourself to see it, there are areas where your wife is smarter and/or more talented than you.

Oops!

Our kids are also not our robots to be programmed or controlled; we're supposed to nurture them so they'll desire to live God-honoring lives and to fulfill God's original intention for them.

As parents, we have no God-given right to traumatize our children into submission. We discipline by maintaining a positive, God-honoring environment in our homes, in good times and bad. We are not our children's masters—God is. God instructs parents to guide and train children in *His* ways, so when they're grown they won't depart from Him (Prov. 22:6). Our calling as parents is to love, help, and encourage our kids to become all they were designed to be in the Lord. Your goal is to provide an environment that equips them to leave you and do the same for their kids. Keep in mind that you may need them to take care of you one day. If they don't understand this concept of nurturing environments, you may find yourself living in the garage when you get old. Ouch!

> God wants you to create environments that provide the same opportunity for others that God has provided for you.

God wants you to create environments that provide the same opportunity for others that God has provided for you.

Authority Test

As God's image bearer, you can't help but be moved by the same things that move God. Your conscience is aware of the care our God-given authority is supposed to provide. If God gives you a child, a dog, or a cat, He's saying, "Your responsibility is to provide a nurturing, caring environment for that child or pet to ensure that they always have what they need to live as I have created them to live."

Violence and cruelty to any living thing is appalling, and you don't need to take a special class in ethics to know that.

Your conscience has already spoken to you, because you have been designed as God's moral mirror, and part of our moral responsibility is to protect the life-giving and image-nurturing environment God created in the first place. God's love and intent are not reflected in an animal's mangled flesh or a child's black eye. You and I have been given His authority to develop and maintain environments that promote the health and God-ordained intention for all of creation. This moral standard, consistent with His design for all things, is deeply embedded in us. All else is unnatural.

Hug a Thug

In the rebuilt Biscailuz Correctional Center in Los Angeles, the inmates who have been convicted of domestic violence crimes serve their time in an unconventional prison environment. They are placed in a program of rehabilitation for batterer intervention. The inmates walk on clean carpets. The men take part in classes and workshops in anger management, addiction prevention, and violence prevention all day long, five days a week, for six weeks to help them understand and change the behaviors that devastated their lives and landed them in prison. These classes are held in nice clean rooms that resemble something in a community college.

The Biscailuz program has no reports of assaults against staff or inmates, and no racial tensions. There are no stabbings, riots, acts of revenge, or other acts of violence that are common occurrences in other institutions. "They respect us here," one inmate said of the low-stress environment, "and the feeling is mutual." The probation program includes continual counseling, evening classes, and assistance in making restitution. Today over 2,000 United States courts are following drug and alcohol rehabilitation programs focused on recovery and rehabilitating addicts rather than just simply locking them up in cells.

In San Quentin State Prison, felons with sentences as harsh as life without parole are given the opportunity to receive their associate's degree by attending classes taught by volunteer professors. These volunteer teachers claim that the prisoners in this program are more polite, respectful, and motivated than regular college students because, as one teacher said, "these men are not taking their learning for granted." As of this writing, well over a hundred San Quentin prisoners have graduated with their Associate of Arts degrees, and many more now continue their college studies after release. Recidivism (repeat offence) among these prisoners is less than 10 percent compared to 61 percent of other inmates. Research shows that the more education a prisoner has, the less likely he or she is to return to prison.

These programs show us that when God-given authority is used to provide nurturing environments for people, they are more likely to live God-honoring lives.

One inmate who spent over thirty years in and out of jail went through the prison rehabilitation program initiated in Boulder, Colorado, and today he is back in society and holds a full-time job. He has paid back $20,000 in restitution owed for his previous crimes, and now he leads programs helping addicts stay clean and sober. He says, "I'm a different person now. I'm the person that I probably always wanted to be." The closer we live in a way that is consistent with the way God designed His image in us to operate, the more fulfilled we will be. Even though, in reality, the inmate needs a spiritual transformation in order to become the person God created him to be, his comment reflects the fact that he has gotten a little taste of what living right is all about, and it felt good. Sometimes people need an opportunity and some instruction on how to be nice, forgiving, and loving. God has given us the authority and responsibility to create these environments wherever we can.

The next time you are confronted with someone you think is rude or prideful, take a minute and express a little extra patience and grace toward him or her and see if it makes a difference in how they respond.

Personal Dominion

Growing up in New York, I learned that if I wanted something, I had to have an "If you don't *take* it, you won't *get* it" mentality. People in New York, especially in the City where I spent a lot of time, have a "go-go-go, get outta my way, I got business to take care of" approach to life. I had to be an assertive, confident person with a purpose in order to survive and keep ahead of things.

I'm a naturally blunt and assertive guy anyway, so when you combine those two attributes with the New York mentality, I sometimes come off as rough. This was most evident when I moved to California, where most people are easygoing and laid-back. Consequently, I rubbed a lot of people the wrong way and didn't realize it until a friend of mine who happens to be a counselor asked me a powerful question: "Do you have any idea how people experience you?"

Hmm. That was a good question. I thought, "No. I don't know how people experience me, and being from New York, I don't care!" But I thought about it and decided I needed to get in touch with my sensitive Christian side, so I had to stop and think about the impression I gave people. (But only when I am in California. Ha!)

Let me ask you the same question. How do people experience you? Do you inspire people? Do you encourage them to enlarge their dreams and think big, or to feel good about themselves? Do people leave your presence motivated to fulfill the purpose God has given them, or is their bubble of hope deflated? Have you ever heard people mumbling criticisms as they walk away from you? If so, that's not a good sign.

Just as we're responsible to live consistent with God's original intent by establishing and exercising authority over environments, so we need to exercise authority over ourselves, our attitudes, and our behavior. We create environments with our attitudes and behaviors, and God has given us the ability to monitor ourselves. Psychologist Daniel Goleman calls this ability to identify and monitor our emotions Emotional Intelligence, or EI.

How does this work?

We've been created with several types of intelligence. We have logical, reasoning intelligence to help us process information and make decisions; we have musical intelligence to discern musical sounds, to create, enjoy, and be inspired by music. We have social intelligence to get along with people; physical intelligence for sports; and linguistic intelligence to think in words and communicate thought. But we also have *emotional intelligence*. This is different from interpersonal intelligence and reasoning intelligence. It's our ability to be aware of how our actions impact other people and how their words and actions impact us.

God has given us the responsibility to possess and maintain a personal presence and environment around us that encourages others to want to fulfill their God-given purpose. Let me challenge you to take time to examine and monitor your attitudes, words, and actions. Listen to yourself. More important, pay attention to the influence you have on the people around you. If you can exercise God-honoring authority over your own personal environment, you'll be far better equipped to exercise God-honoring authority over other environments.

You can reject your God-given authority, of course, but when you understand and act on the authority God has given you as His image bearer, you will see more of Him in you, as well as in those whose lives you've influenced.

10

Authority Taker

All about Me

The young girl's face is swollen, scarred, and bruised. She's thinking of her room at home, her collection of Barbies and Beanie Babies packed away in boxes in her closet. Just last week she had an argument with her mother. "I'm fourteen years old now," she screamed. "I'm giving away all this kid stuff in my room—the Dora the Explorer comforter and my Small World and Bratz dolls." She was a teenager now, no longer a little girl. Her mother's reply was, "Baby, you'll always be my little girl."

But now Keisha's hands are tied and bleeding as she lies on an old mattress that belongs in a dumpster. If she makes too much noise, she will get beat again. And then another man comes in. She has stopped counting the men. They all remind her of her teachers at school, the fathers in her neighborhood, someone's grandpa.

She had been walking home from school with her best friend Taylor when two guys drove up in a nice car. They asked where the girls were heading. Keisha and Taylor were flattered that older boys were flirting with them. They giggled, rolled their eyes. Keisha thought the guys were cute, but they both knew better than to get in a car with strangers, so they kept walking. It happened so fast. The young man on the passenger side jumped out, grabbed Keisha around the neck, and pulled her into the car. Taylor took off running.

How long had she been chained to the bed? How many days and nights hungry, hurting, bleeding, sick? They took off the handcuffs only to let her out to wash, use the toilet, and then—the men, the men. Were there other girls like her kept in this place? She thought she saw two girls about ten years old in the bathroom yesterday. Matted hair, vacant eyes, bruised like her, but then the door closed, and Keisha wondered if she had imagined them. She thought of her room at home, her ballerina lamp, her mother's hugs, "You'll always be my baby . . ."

The number of children and women trafficked as sex slaves internationally has purportedly reached 27 million. The sex slavery trade is one of the great evils of humanity. Keisha is another statistic in the unthinkable business of child sex trade. Most of the young girls and boys don't make it out alive. Fortunately she was rescued from that lifestyle.

God gave us His authority so we would promote the original purpose of everything He created—namely, the image of God in people. *Authority takers* develop environments that muzzle and destroy the development of the image of God in people. In this chapter, we'll focus on how we can recognize the effects of authority takers.

Environment Killer

The infamous murder case of Casey Anthony, the mother who was on trial for the murder of her two-year-old child,

Caylee, became an international scandal in 2011 when the jury pronounced the verdict: not guilty. It shocked and outraged most of the world, who believed it was obvious that Casey Anthony, allegedly unstable and self-absorbed, murdered the little girl whose adorable face was posted daily all over the media for over three years. The child's mother gave the impression of total disregard for the death of her daughter. The reason there was such widespread hatred for Casey Anthony is because, as an authority taker, she violated *the universal conscience every human has* about our God-given responsibility to create a nurturing environment for our children.

A loving, safe environment for a child is the first calling of a parent. The responsibilities to nurture, encourage, bless, protect, teach, and assist a child to reach his or her God-given purpose in life are what it means to be a parent. We are supposed to do what we can to give others the best opportunity to thrive. We are to give people the tools and resources for the potential of their God image to be fulfilled.

Authority takers kill the nurturing environment we're responsible to create for those around us, not only as parents, but also as teachers, pastors, employees, and friends. Our Father in heaven never gave human beings dominion over other *human beings*. That's called slavery. He gave humans the authority to take care of and nurture their environment.

Authority Taker Test

Authority from God is a free gift. Authority is something God gave us from the beginning. We receive His authority as a person receives a gift. It's granted to us graciously by God, though we've done nothing to earn it. We were created to be givers, not takers, and especially not takers of others' physical,

> We were created to be givers, not takers, and especially not takers of others' physical, emotional, and spiritual freedom.

emotional, and spiritual freedom. On the other hand, authority *takers* are just that: takers of all the things that help people grow and develop.

Authority takers are people who reach for either more authority than God originally intended for them, or they apply authority over things that God never intended for them to take. You can't take authority from *God*, but you can take it from a *person*. Any time you pull a person down, steal from or disrespect him or her, you're taking authority that doesn't belong to you.

When our God image becomes *blurred*, it's because we've lost sight of who we are, and in whose image we're created. "People should do exactly what I want them to! Do what it takes to get ahead! Don't let anyone stop you! You can be rich!" If we entertain such thoughts, we'll feed the thoughts with actions, and the damage will be great. Recognize these signs:

- You're a taker if you take another person's right to enjoy life.
- You're a taker if you're rude, selfish, domineering, and think you have the right to be.
- You're a taker if you order someone to do what you want and get furious when they don't do it.
- You're a taker if you bully someone and destroy their sense of peace. As an I AM imposter, you feel entitled to take from others and hold them down.
- You're a taker if you dominate attention in a group and have to be the center of it all.
- You're a taker if you do all the talking and don't let anyone else get a word in edgewise.

- You're a taker if you see your children as a hindrance, holding you back from having the life you'd like to have.
- You're a taker if you only hang out with people you can control.

A blurred sense of our God-given authority stems from the blurred sense of who we are as unique individuals. If you're an authority taker, you think you have the right to do whatever you want at anyone's expense, and it's your right to dominate and even possess other people's lives. How else can anyone enslave innocent children and women or commit murder?

Opportunity Thief

At the end of my NFL career and the beginning of my youth ministry career, I began conducting high school assemblies. These assemblies were the most nerve-wracking but exciting speaking engagements. The auditoriums would be packed with as many as 3,500 students. On a morning after one of these assemblies, as the kids were leaving the gym, a student ran toward me with tears in his eyes. He yelled, "Tell me I can play football! Tell me I can play football!"

I turned to him.

"Tell me I'm not too short," he yelled.

He told me his dad said he was too short to play football. "Tell me I'm big enough!" he pleaded.

Based on that limited information about this kid, it seemed like he lived in an environment that was holding him down, filling his head and heart with nothing but doubt about himself. It appeared that his father didn't create an environment that fostered the growth and development of his son's God image. (I say "it appeared" because his father may have had a good reason to hold his son back from playing football, but the boy's height had nothing to do with it. One of the best football players on my San Diego Charger team was a running back who was only 5'6".)

People who are under the influence of authority takers will feel like they're not allowed to dream or create and take risks. They feel like they are being held back, and their God-given dreams are being stifled. Do you think it is possible that *you* could be an authority taker? Could it be possible that the people you regularly come in contact with feel like you hold them back or cause them to doubt themselves? Keep in mind, any negative thoughts about yourself only come from the devil, and it is those thoughts and perspectives that authority takers project and express to others. Does that describe you?

Self-Dominion

I was approached by a married couple who were struggling with a unique situation in their relationship. They stood in front of me, hugging each other, crying and smiling all at the same time. There were happy tears and frustrated tears. They had both cheated on each other and had forgiven each other, but they couldn't forgive themselves. They were being crushed by their own guilt and couldn't set themselves free to receive what God has given them. Forgiveness.

When God tells us that we need to *love our neighbor as we love ourselves*, it implies that we need to love ourselves. How do we do that? We look at how God loves us, and *that* is how we are to love ourselves. He is forgiving, kind, compassionate, understanding, patient, and always seeking the best in us.

Think about it. If your love for yourself is critical, judgmental, and unforgiving, your love for others will be critical, judgmental, and unforgiving. If your love for yourself is stingy and selfish, your love for others will be stingy and selfish. If your love for yourself is something you feel you must earn, then your love for others will be something you feel they must earn. Before you can love someone else in a way that is uplifting and encouraging, you need to love yourself in the same way; but if you have adopted the self-defeating names that Satan has given you, always questioning your self-worth, your love for others will never mirror God's love for them.

Every year in San Diego County, over 400 people successfully take their lives. That's more than one suicide per day in our city. Suicide is the ultimate act of hopelessness and the symbol of living in an *authority taker environment*. One of the reasons people commit suicide is because they're convinced that nothing will remove their pain and suffering, and they can't see beyond the present moment. They embrace the age-old lie of the devil: "The world will be a better place without me." They see themselves trapped with no hope of relief, when in truth there's hope all around. They can find hope in the help that friends, family, and clergy are willing to provide.

Let me reiterate the question asked earlier in the book. How do you impact the lives of other people?

And here's another important question to ask yourself: How is *your* life being impacted by other people?

Authority takers are constantly striving to prove their identity. They create environments that beat everyone else down. Most often people who hurt others are hurting the most. These I AM imposters who become authority takers feel the need to be something God didn't create them to be. They're always falling short, so they feel like they're failures. They have to beat others down to feel good about themselves.

Gossip is a common expression of that. Gossip is a cowardly way of pulling someone down behind his or her back. But you must keep in mind that you cannot pull someone down unless you are below him or her, or at least you perceive yourself to be below them. How often do you find yourself trying to pull someone down with your words?

Whether you're an authority taker or your life is surrounded by authority takers, it's critical to begin changing your environment and seeing yourself through God's eyes. If you are a victim to the kind of environment that authority takers produce, hope is closer than you think. Let me assure you, you can get out of it.

> Whether you're an authority taker or your life is surrounded by authority takers, it's critical to begin changing your environment.

It Only Takes a Few . . .

A restaurant owner wanted to begin serving a specialty dish of frog legs. He went on a search for nice plump frogs, and he heard about a guy ten miles outside of town who owned a pond full of frogs. He went to see the pond. As he approached the pond, all he could hear was the croaking of frogs, and the closer he got, the more clearly he could visualize his smiling customers eating his delicious frog legs.

He was so excited, he worked out a deal with the owner of the pond to not only buy all the frogs but the pond itself, sight unseen. Soon after the purchase, the restaurant owner drained the pond, expecting to find hundreds of frogs. He was shocked to find there were only five frogs in the pond making all that noise.

The negative, lying thoughts you have about yourself are like that pond. You think there are a whole lot more frogs than there really are. We usually have a lot less critics than we think. What you hear in your head is never as bad as the reality. How you respond to drama, criticism, and gossip is an indication of the information you are focusing on. That's why it is critical to make a distinction between *information* and *truth*.

Information could be someone's criticism of you. They may make fun of your big feet or your weight or the car you drive. Then Satan will add fuel to the fire with more information and tell you that you are less than, a failure, or a loser. If you focus on that information, it is understandable that you would respond by pulling others down to feel better about yourself. It would be understandable based on that information, if it were true, to develop environments or develop a living space designed to promote your self-image at the expense of others. But, and there is always a but, instead of focusing on INFORMATION, you need to focus on the TRUTH.

Those personal characteristics that people make fun of do not make you less lovable. As a matter of fact, the big feet, crooked nose, or squinty eyes that you have are only a few of the thousands of qualities that make you unique and special. The *truth* is how God, your Creator, feels about you and the one-of-a-kind plans He has for the one-of-a-kind person you are. The *truth* is the unconditional love He has for you and His desire to express that love to you.

What about You?

Do you believe the negative lies the devil has drilled into your head? Let me encourage you to look for an authority taker attitude in yourself and also the people you allow into your life. Ask yourself if you're surrounded by people who lift you up or beat you down. Choose positive people in your life!

Make a decision to be an encourager to the people in your life, and it won't be long before God begins to see more of Himself in the way you are exercising His authority in your life.

11

Authority Possessor

Image Consultant

Mr. Authority

One afternoon, as I drove my daughter Kelly to her ballet class with a friend of mine sitting in the backseat, Kelly turned to me and said, "Daddy, I want to buy my friend a birthday present."

I wondered what this had to do with me, so I said, "And?"

I heard her huff and puff, and before she blew the house down, she said, finally, "Well, can I have some money?"

I looked over at her serious little face. "How much?"

Without hesitation, she said, "Forty dollars."

I said, "Oooh! Is your friend's name Mommy?"

Another huff and puff. "No, Dad!"

"Oh! It's for me!"

"No, Dad. It's for a new friend. I just met her."

> Jesus Christ has given us His spiritual authority for one simple reason: to fulfill the Lord's Prayer on earth, where we live right now.

My daughter is a very giving person, but the only problem is that she's always giving with my money. I said, "How about twenty dollars?"

She said, "How about thirty-five?"

I said, "How about twenty?"

"How about thirty?"

"Twenty."

"Thirty!"

We went back and forth, and then my friend in the backseat leaned forward and said, "Hey Kelly, why don't you just ask your dad for his credit card?"

DUDE?

With that little card my daughter would possess more buying power than she ever had in her life. She'd have the *authority* to make purchases she could never make on her own.

In this chapter we'll see how and why Jesus, the One who has *all* authority over heaven and earth, will restore to *us* the full amount of spiritual authority He originally intended us to exercise. We'll see how He gives us His credit card to use with His name on it.

Jesus Christ has given us His spiritual authority for one simple reason: to fulfill the Lord's Prayer on earth, where we live right now.

Boss Lady

When I was in high school, I was not a big fan of reading but loved numbers and science. As a result, I became interested in engineering (and my girlfriend's dad just happened to have an engineering firm in New York City). At sixteen he gave me a job as an intern at his firm in Manhattan, and my goal on day one was to learn what my job was and who my boss would be. That person was a woman named Shirley. She immediately gave me packages to deliver, the first one to an address in Brooklyn. Having grown up in Long Island twenty-one miles outside of Manhattan, I didn't know anything about getting around the five boroughs of the City by train. Delivering a package from Manhattan to Brooklyn meant I'd have to take two or three trains. I asked Shirley how to get to the address in Brooklyn, and she pointed toward Sixth Avenue. "The subway's on the corner, figure it out."

Even though I was hired as an intern (to learn about engineering, I thought), I spent most of my time as a gofer: a same-day delivery boy, delivering mail and running errands.

Shirley said that she'd be the one who'd be giving me my assignments each day. She told me she'd give me petty cash when I needed it and time off when I'd earned it. If I had a problem with someone, I was to come to her. She was a strong black woman from the Bronx, and you do not mess with strong black women from the Bronx. Shirley was also the coolest person in the building.

So it was Shirley I was accountable to. Shirley had the authority to tell me to go left or to go right. She had the authority to tell me when to get to work and when to leave, and she gave *me* the authority to do my job.

When it comes to your spiritual life, who has authority over your life's purpose? Who has the authority to tell you to go left or right? Who has authority to answer your prayers? Who has the spiritual authority to empower you to live a victorious life? Who has the authority to reestablish a deep, abiding relationship between you and God? And if I told you who had that much authority over your life and the world, would you submit to Him?

Would you trust Him?

The Bible says that *Jesus* is the One who has authority over all things, both natural and spiritual. In Matthew 28:18, Jesus says, "All authority has been given to Me in heaven and on earth." Jesus holds the power of eternal life. In John 17:2, He speaks to the Father about Himself, "For you granted him [Jesus] authority over all people that he might give eternal life to all those you have given him" (NIV).

One way to be sure about Jesus's authority is to look at His life on earth and what He accomplished while He was here.

Proof of Authority

During my second year in the NFL, I walked into the office of my position coach and asked for more playing time. We had to learn about forty different plays each week, so there was a very significant mental aspect of the game in addition to the obvious physical component. I felt like I was making plays in practice both mentally and physically, and I figured I should have more playing time.

My coach sat quietly as I pleaded my case, and then he said, "Miles, if you keep doing the right things on the field, your play will speak so loud that you don't have to say anything to me."

Jesus's authority, as the Bible shows us, was given to Him by the Father, and it was evident by His life and what He did. He said, "If I do not do the works of My Father, do not believe Me, but if I do, though you do not believe Me, believe the works, that you may know and believe that the Father is in Me and I in Him" (John 10:37–38). John said there were so many things that Jesus did, "if they were written one by one, I suppose that even the world itself could not contain the books that would be written" (John 21:25).

Here are just *some* of the miracles Jesus performed while He was on earth:

- He turned water into wine at the wedding of Cana (John 2:9).
- He healed all sick, broken, and infirm people who came to Him (Isa. 53:5).
- He cast out demons from people (Mark 1:26; Matt. 12:29).
- He multiplied fish for fishermen (Luke 5:6; John 21:6).
- He fed 5,000 people with five loaves and two fishes (Matt. 14:19–21).
- He fed 4,000 with seven loaves and few fish and had food left over (Matt. 15:36–38).
- He raised the dead (Luke 7:14–15; Matt. 9:18; Mark 5:42; Luke 8:54–55; John 11).
- He calmed a violent storm at sea (Matt. 8:26).
- He gave the blind sight (Matt. 9:27–30).
- He cleansed the lepers (Matt. 8:3; Mark 1:41; Luke 5:13).
- He healed the deaf and dumb (Mark 7:33–35).
- He walked on the sea (Matt. 14:25).
- He rose from the dead (Luke 24:6–7; John 10:18) and afterward walked the earth for forty days (Acts 1:3).
- He changed and goes on changing hearts, giving new purpose to lives (Luke 19:2–10).
- He brought the kingdom of God to earth (John 3:3; (Matt. 12:28).

Jesus's authority empowered Him (and therefore you and me) to say to a disease, "Be gone!" He proclaimed physical deformities be fixed and tumultuous storms be quieted and turned into sunny days. He commanded the spiritual forces of darkness to set people free from bondage. But *how* did

Jesus do these miracles? How was He able to exercise such unheard of authority over disease, demons, life, and even death? Most of all, how are His deeds of two thousand years ago impacting *your* life now?

Jesus came to restore a heaven-like attitude in your heart and mind, your relationships, and how you care for the world He created. Jesus teaches through the Lord's Prayer that His authority is intended to restore earth to a heavenly existence. He came to replace the hatred in hearts with love. He came to replace fear with hope, impatience with patience, discouragement with encouragement.

Let's be clear: He's not *giving* us His authority, He's *exercising it through us*. You were created to be a main conduit of Jesus's authority. Do you find yourself exercising authority in situations with the belief that it is yours to exercise in the way you see fit? Remember, He fits in us like a hand in a glove for the purpose of fulfilling his plan *in* and *through* our lives.

> You were created to be a main conduit of Jesus's authority.

My daughter thought my friend's suggestion about the credit card made sense, so she asked, all wide-eyed, "Daddy, why don't you just let me use your credit card?" As the words were coming out of her mouth, her hand reached for the card. Unfortunately, she didn't realize that she couldn't use the card without me being there in person. My name is on the card. You can't use the power and authority of God unless Jesus is there Himself, simply because it's not *us using His power* with Him at the checkout alongside us, it's *He Himself* exercising *His authority through us*. Jesus's power and authority isn't lent to us to be used in His presence; it's actually used by Him in our presence.

I know you're thinking, "DUH! Of course!" But let's be honest, how many times have you forgotten this and thought to yourself, "Wow, *I'm* really something. Look at *my* skills." And, "Oh, *I'm* sure anointed." Be honest with yourself. Have you ever thought, "People really listen to *me*!" "*I'm* really good. Yes, *I've* got what it takes." Me Me Me—and not *He He He.*

Just as your arm reaches to grab something with your hand, Jesus extends His authority through your hands and blesses people. He extends His authority through your prayers, and He pushes mountains until they topple. He reaches through our heart into the hearts of others when we are teaching or sharing our faith. We must be reminded of this, lest we think that *we're* the ones who change lives.

Throughout the Bible we see the Holy Spirit performing over-the-top miracles. People will tell me at an altar call that they felt like I was speaking directly to them. Well, I didn't even know these people. It was God Himself speaking to their hearts through a preacher. "Not by might nor by power, but by my Spirit, says the LORD Almighty" (Zech. 4:6 NIV).

The apostles preached, performed miracles, and lived powerful lives of faith because they were filled with the Holy Spirit of God, as Jesus was. Acts 4:29–30 says that *the hand of the Lord* performed signs and wonders! In Acts 5:38–39 Gamaliel rightfully tells his peers that to oppose the apostles would be to oppose God Himself. It was *God Himself* acting through the apostles.

So when Ephesians 6:10 tells us, "Finally, my brethren, be strong in the Lord and in the power of His might," it's not only His strength and might we're to be strong in, but Jesus Himself who exercises His strength and might in us. This very simple fact helps give context to how we should expect to access and use God's authority.

Jesus told His disciples before He was crucified, "Very truly, I tell you, it is for your good that I am going away. Unless I go away, the Advocate [Holy Spirit] will not Come to you; but if I go, I will send him to you" (John 16:7 NIV). Jesus gave us His Holy Spirit to live in us and accomplish the work He assigns us. All that we do in His name has to be consistent with Who He is, His character, and His name.

A young man had a mad crush on a girl he barely knew in his Bible class. He completely believed that one day they'd get married. He was so convinced it was God's plan that he walked up and told her that she was supposed to marry him. Of course she thought he was crazy. He told her that, because he prayed daily in Jesus's name, they'd get married one day—it was bound to happen. He even quoted Scripture to her!

Sound ridiculous? It *is* ridiculous. Here was a guy who thought he could pray for anything he wanted, and as long as he said "In Jesus's name" at the end of his prayer, like magic, he'd get what he asked for. Praying in Jesus's name does not ensure that you'll get what you ask for. Yes, Jesus did tell us in John 14:13–14: "And whatever you ask in My name, that I will do, that the Father may be glorified in the Son. If you ask anything in My name, I will do it." He actually meant something different from what many would like to think. When you pray in the name of Jesus, what you're actually saying to God is, "God, grant my request if it's according to Your will and for Your glory, not mine. God, grant my requests only if it helps me fulfill Your plan for my life. If my prayer is contrary to Your purpose for me, please do not grant it."

A more accurate (and Holy Spirit–led) prayer for the young man with marriage on his mind might have been, "Lord, I'm really attracted to this girl, but I only want Your will in my life. I only want her as my wife if it is according to *Your* will, not my will."

When you call on Jesus's name in prayer, you're accessing His authority for the purpose of fulfilling *His* plan in your life. When you pray in Jesus's name, you are requesting God to exercise His authority through you *only if your request matches His plan for heaven on earth in your life or in the situation at hand.*

The Holy Spirit prompts us to pray for the purpose of glorifying God. Don't waste your time asking Him to exercise His authority on things that are incompatible with His plan and character. The Holy Spirit prompts us to pray for the purpose of glorifying God. He didn't give us His power and authority for whatever we wanted. It is completely for His glory and benefit and good pleasure.

Acts 1:8 tells us that when we receive the Holy Spirit, we would receive power, the ability and authority to get things done, but not for our own purposes. Jesus says the power is so we can be His witnesses in Jerusalem, Judea, Samaria, and the ends of the earth. These four places represent concentric circles that spread to the whole world. He's saying, in other words, "I have a plan for that power and authority, and if you use it according to My plan, I will trust you with more of it."

We shouldn't think that just because we have Christ in our life we can exercise authority in any way or any situation we want. We each have a unique design and specific purpose, and He'll guide and focus you if you pray for His will. There are some situations where you'll be assigned to exercise more authority than in other situations. There'll be ministry opportunities that you'll try to get involved in that just don't seem to work out, and it's because He hasn't ordained His authority in you to be exercised in that manner. It's critical to not only know the authority you have but also where it belongs to honor Him best.

The most convincing evidence that you're submitted to God's authority is when people see God alive and real in your life. If He created you for the purpose of seeing Himself in you, why shouldn't people *expect* to see Him in your life?

When was the last time you said something that you wished you hadn't said, and for days after you kicked yourself for not having enough authority over your mouth to stop it? Your weakness controls you instead of you controlling your weakness. It is one thing to have access to God's authority, but quite another to submit to it.

During my cocaine days, I would look at myself in the mirror and say, "Don't put that white powder in your nose." Then I would go right ahead and sniff it up my nose. The cocaine had authority over my life. It wasn't until I surrendered cocaine's authority to Jesus that I was able to stop, and I did in one day.

In the middle of a mini-argument with my wife while both of us were gritting our teeth, the doorbell rang. On my way to answer the door, I had to get control of myself quick because the little kids from up the block were coming to sell candy for their Little League team. I opened the door and saw nothing but their little toothless smiles and their big eyes looking up at me as they held out boxes of candy the size of their little bodies. I couldn't help but smile, whether I felt like it or not. All of a sudden I was grinning, talking nice, being patient. My anger melted, and I was able to take charge of my feelings and attitudes.

We can take the authority Jesus gives us over our bad attitudes, anger, and lack of control over our emotions. I made my feelings and attitude my slave in that moment. The *presence* of Jesus's authority in our hearts is one thing, but we must each day and hour and minute submit our attitudes, actions, and issues to Him and make them *His* slaves. There are times that we actually choose to stay mad or frustrated because we think we deserve to be mad. Have you ever stayed mad so you can punish the person who made you mad? God's authority has set us free so we can choose to surrender our selfishness and take control of those attitudes just like I did when the kids came to my door.

God has given you access to the authority to take dominion over your urges of anger, sexual cravings, addictions, or anything else that feels like handcuffs keeping you in bondage. He wants you free as much as you want to be free.

The next time you're tempted to forget who and whose you are, immediately surrender your thoughts, actions, and attitudes to the authority of Christ. Imagine that He is standing right next to you with a huge, loving smile on His face, telling you, "I love you. Trust Me."

The Po Po

One afternoon I was driving down the freeway in the speed lane when all of a sudden, the Po Po (police) was right behind me. His lights weren't flashing, there was no siren; he was just following me. I immediately looked down to see how fast I was going. My heart started pounding and I began to sweat. What should I do? Change lanes? Slow down? If that has ever happened to you, you might have been tempted to put your foot on the brake, but that's probably the last thing you should do. Your red brake lights will say, just go ahead and give me a ticket. Instead, just take your foot off the gas and let your car naturally slow down, which is what I did. Of course, change lanes and let the nice police officer pass you.

The presence of the police car behind me represented the law. Right, wrong, ticket or no ticket, we're reminded of the speed limit and the consequences of breaking the law. So often, if the police are out of sight, thinking about the law is out of sight. The presence of the police car behind us is a reminder of the law and the consequences of breaking it.

Because we don't see God, we can easily forget about His laws and His guidelines for life, and we tend to ignore His Word. The Holy Spirit's presence in our lives acts like the flashing lights of the police car, reminding us and encouraging us to remember who we are in Christ and to obey Him, even when we think He's not watching us.

Whenever Jesus walked up to a demon-possessed person, He didn't have to announce Himself; the demons knew exactly who He was. In the eighth chapter of Matthew, two demon-possessed men rushed out of their cave screaming, "What have we to do with you, Jesus, You Son of God?" They had never met Jesus before. And Mark 3:11 reports, "And the unclean spirits, whenever they saw Him, fell down before Him and cried out, saying, 'You are the Son of God.'"

Christ's authority puts all evil demonic forces on notice that there's a new sheriff in town. They must submit to His authority. When God's authority is actively exercised, it *will have impact on the spiritual forces in the lives of the people with whom you come in contact.* But again, this will be in proportion to your level of submission to that authority. God has given you authority over the evil forces of darkness to be used at His discretion and according to His will.

> God has given you authority over the evil forces of darkness.

While I was ministering in Mexico at a medical clinic, a girl was brought to me who had an ear defect that prevented her from hearing. Jesus has authority over all defects, but whether He was going to exercise it through me at that time was a mystery. The timing and manner in which He exercises His authority are above my pay grade to understand.

But what was my concern—or more, *His* concern—was whether or not I'd submit myself to His direction and authority to establish His will on earth as it is in heaven. I was considering placing my fingers in her ears and praying for her like Jesus did in Mark 7:33–35, but how might that look? Would people think it was weird? (I believe people fail to access His authority many times because of their own insecurity.)

I had to have the faith to ask to put my fingers in her ears and pray. I had to obey and exercise that authority by asking if I could pray for the child, and I did. I placed my fingers in her ears and prayed. She looked at me with a funny expression and then walked away. Nothing seemed to have happened. But her healing was totally up to God, not up to me or anyone else.

About thirty minutes later during an examination by a doctor, it was revealed that the child's physical deformity was gone. Her ears were restored.

We have more authority over the spiritual forces of darkness than we know! As we submit to Christ, He exercises His authority *through us* to bring heaven to earth in each situation. Remind yourself to exercise your God-given authority over the forces of evil in your life and the lives of others. The more you surrender yourself, your thoughts, and your desires to Him, the more authority He will exercise through your life.

Psalm 37:4 says that if you delight yourself in the Lord, He will give you the desires of your heart. The more your life is transformed into the image of Christ, the more you'll find yourself desiring what God desires. You'll have a hunger and thirst for what God wants for you, and a mind for what's on His mind. The more this happens, the more likely your intent for His authority will match His intent. The more trustworthy you become with God's authority and power, the more of His authority and power He will entrust to you.

The parable of the talents in Matthew 25 says if you're faithful in little, He will trust you with more. When God is confident that you can use His authority the way He would use it, and to promote His purposes, He can trust you with true riches and opportunities to impact lives of other people.

12

Authority Magnifier

The Gospel of Hope

Seven years after we started The Rock Church, my staff and I decided to hire a church consulting service to help us organize a strategic plan for our church. To start the conversation, the consultant asked us what I thought at the time was a *duh* question. She asked us, "What is the objective for your Sunday services?" We all shifted in our seats, thinking maybe she'd never consulted at a church before.

As an evangelist, I responded, "Evangelism." Someone else said, "Teaching," another said, "Worship," and another said, "Encouragement." The lady wrote our answers on the board and then explained that, yes, all of these were good, but the number one purpose for Sunday church services is to bring people into the *presence of God*.

"People don't need more information about God, and they aren't just looking for an opportunity to sing to or about God;

they're looking for a *personal encounter with God Himself*," she said. "Don't get me wrong—singing to and about God can *facilitate* a God encounter, but it's God *Himself* we need, not the song."

When God gave us authority over the earth, He granted us authority to create environments in which opportunities for His purposes can be fulfilled. In this chapter, we'll learn that the most powerful expression of authority given to the church is to create an environment that brings people into the presence of God. We do this both corporately and individually.

At the dedication ceremony of Solomon's temple, the glory of the Lord filled the temple so completely the priests couldn't perform their duties. "And it came to pass, when the priests came out of the holy place, that the cloud filled the house of the LORD, so that the priests could not continue ministering because of the cloud; for the glory of the LORD filled the house of the LORD." (1 Kings 8:10–11).

The same thing happened when Moses dedicated the tabernacle in the wilderness: The cloud of glory covered the tabernacle and the glory of the Lord filled it. Moses wasn't able to enter the tabernacle, because the cloud rested above it, and the glory of the Lord filled the tabernacle (Exod. 40:34). God wanted His people to have a personal encounter with Him.

A few months after I accepted the Lord as my Savior, my wife and I went to a nondenominational church for the first time in my life as a Christian. The church was in an old San Diego movie theatre with about seven hundred seats. We sat in the back row of a packed house, and three minutes or so into the service I started crying. I kept raising my eyebrows to stop the tears from rolling, but my eyes kept welling up. I thought, "Why am I crying?"

Then, *boom*, it hit me. Was it the singing? It wasn't the sound of the voices necessarily, but something spiritually loving that was washing over me. For the first time in my life, I was having a *real God experience in a church*. Church is the one and only place that has as its primary function to facilitate a personal meeting with God. This happens when the church worships God in spirit and in truth.

I see people in church all the time with their hands raised and words coming out their mouths, but they are not worshiping. Worship is much more than singing or going through some motions. Worship happens when your soul—the immaterial, nonphysical, eternal aspect of who you are—reaches toward God like a child reaches up for a parent.

The reason I was crying in the church was because, on a spiritual level, I resonated with what everyone was doing, what the music was guiding us to do, and what the atmosphere had facilitated our souls to do: to reach up to and connect with God. The sound, lights, music, lyrics, and actions of the people were all focused on connecting with God.

Living Water

The Mississippi River is over 2,300 miles long and runs from Minnesota to the Gulf of Mexico. It starts out as narrow as 40 feet and can get as wide as 21 miles. The smaller rivers and streams that pour into the Mississippi come from 31 states. They're like dozens of baby snakes all crawling toward the big mama snake. These baby snakes represent the many aspects of our souls, the nonphysical, eternal part of a person that communicates and connects directly with God. They're our desires, our wills, our dreams and aspirations. They're our imagination, emotions, and thoughts.

It's our *soul* that magnifies the Lord (Luke 1:46). The different functions and abilities of our soul represent a different stream or smaller river that feeds into our spiritual river of Living Water that flows upstream toward God.

Because our soul is eternal and will outlive the body, it can't live on the same food that the physical body lives on. The soul has different needs and desires. The thirst of our soul can't be quenched with a drink from Starbucks. The need for companionship that our soul craves can't be satisfied with a hug. Our soul is only satisfied with a *God encounter*.

Your soul has the ability to connect with God. It can, on a spiritual level, receive encouragement, wisdom, and insight from God. Your soul has abilities beyond what you can understand. You were created to interact with God in a way that results in receiving everything you're ordained to receive from Him. Your soul knows things your flesh doesn't know, and it can do things your flesh can't do, such as interact with God.

I'm sure there have been countless times in your life when you knew something about a situation without knowing where the information was coming from. It was probably an insight of your soul and spirit, a gift of God that you weren't aware of.

As I said earlier, my brother played QB at Syracuse University. I had the chance to see him play in one home game in person, and unfortunately for me, he only played half of the game. He threw four touchdown passes in the first half, so they took him out at halftime.

Later, Don, our mother, and I were walking back to his dorm when a female student came toward us on the sidewalk. The closer she got to us, the wider her eyes got as she realized who my brother was. (To say that he was the big man on campus was an understatement.) She walked right up to him and said, "You're Don McPherson!" Then she grabbed his nasty, crusty throwing hand and kissed it! Worship is a spontaneous response of respect at the revelation of God. What is your response when you walk into church? Do you require the preacher to entertain you? That's not going to church to worship God, but more like going to the comedy club to be amused.

True worship is when our soul spontaneously flows up toward God. We can't force worship, but we can create an environment that facilitates it. We do that by keeping our thoughts toward God. Singing, reading the Bible, praying, talking about what God is doing in our lives—all of these prime our souls for true worship. When our focus is on God—His faithfulness, His holy character, and His faithful promises—we can't help but worship Him. Our worship becomes intentional and consistent.

Keep in mind that true worship is based on the most compelling truth about who God is, not on what He will do for us. Often we get caught up in focusing our worship on the blessings that come from God's hand versus the love that comes from His heart.

Think about your personal friends. Even though you receive joy and satisfaction being with them, the friends who will be close for life are people you respect—not because of what you get, but because of who they are. In other words, if they became ill, paralyzed, mute, and you could not enjoy them the way you do today, you would still love them as friends because of *who they are*, not what they do or can't do.

Worship Health

The surface of our lungs, nasal passages, and nose are covered with countless tiny hairs called *cilia*. All day and night, they are brushing mucus out of those airways and into the stomach to be eliminated. These cilia keep the body clean by creating this river of mucus that is always moving through our body, taking dirt with it.

Our *spiritual* cilium is represented by the active role we play in directing our soul toward God by our conscious decisions to think about God, to pray to God, to surrender our cares and worries to God, to call on Him for strength, and to tell Him how much we love and appreciate Him.

Since Satan does everything he can to destroy your relationship with God, he works overtime to distract us from worshiping Him. Satan will throw in every distraction he can think of to hinder your God experience, so you have to proactively prepare yourself to worship God.

The cares of the world can distract us and choke out our willingness to seek God. How many times have you been all set to go to church, and then your spouse is late? Or your kids throw up just as you're getting in the car? You're out of gas, or someone cuts in front of you and takes your parking space, or your daughter can't stop crying and won't get in the car because she lost her Justin Bieber bobblehead? Or you walk into church and can't sit in your favorite seat? Satan will do anything to distract you from God and get your soul to flow away from God and the blessing He has for you!

Worship is when we make a decision to direct our lives up to God. The church is designed to create an atmosphere where connecting with God is unavoidable. Hebrews 10:24 speaks of spurring one another on toward love and good deeds. This is what happens in church. In church, we see God and connect with Him. In church, we learn how to enter His presence, so that outside the church building we can do the same. God gave the church the authority to create an environment where people can experience God and learn how to seek Him on their own.

Discouragement can cause us to avoid surrendering our hearts to God. You need to remember that you're in the midst of a spiritual battle designed to hinder your worship and your relationship with God. You can't walk around expecting supernatural God encounters to just flow your way without any effort from you. I admit, you can't force a God experience, but you sure can prepare for it by calling on God, focusing your heart and mind on God, and praying against the impact of Satan's distraction on your life.

Unguarded Heart

One night my wife and I were having ice cream with two of our children when our third child came home. I told the first two to share some of their ice cream with the third child. They both put their arms around their bowls to keep their ice cream to themselves. Some people come to church with arms around their hearts because they don't want to share. They're scared that if they give their heart to God, He's going to make them do something they don't want to do, or maybe He'll make them give something that they don't want to give or be something they don't want to be.

I recently spoke to a wealthy man who was considering making a financial gift to the church, and during the conversation he placed his hands over his heart. He said that he was scared God was going to ask him to do something he might not want to do. I asked him if he trusted God, and he said he did, but he needed help with his unbelief.

Well, there's no doubt God is going ask us to do something we haven't done, give something away that we've never given, and become something we never thought of becoming. But we'll soon realize that God is faithful, and whatever He wants us to do or to give up will become the best thing that ever happened to us.

In all my years of being involved in athletics, one of the most important lessons I learned was the value of warming up before any workout. We would run, stretch, and break a sweat in order to prepare our body for the stress of the workout ahead. This same principle applies to our spiritual life. It's critical to prepare our hearts to seek and meet with God before we jump into worship. There have been many times when I have arrived at church and gotten bombarded with questions, unexpected drama, or last-minute changes, so I developed a habit of sitting in my car for a short period of time before I walk into church. I take this time to settle my heart and mind, and to get focused on God. I remind myself of His faithfulness, His love, and His purpose for my life.

If I'm distracted or have a bad attitude, I'll tell God about it. I'll sit quietly and clear my mind, or I'll start singing or praying. I'll confess the latest junk that is swirling around in my mind and heart and read the Bible. When I'm preparing to worship Him, I want my mind to be clear of everything except the Lord.

In 2011 our church went on a twenty-one-day fast. I knew that a fast was going to stress some people out, but it's necessary for people to be challenged to surrender everything, especially eating, to God. Through fasting, people can experience the blessings of being focused on God.

Some people had a hard time giving up sweets, others had trouble with breads and starches, but probably the biggest challenge was for the coffee drinkers. I know this because just before we started the fast, I asked how many people drank coffee every day, and just about half the congregation raised their hands. I asked how many people had to have a cup of coffee before they started the day, and just about the same number raised their hands. Coffee drinking had trained their bodies and altered their physiology and biology to need the coffee in the morning to wake up and focus. I'm sure God would prefer that, instead of needing coffee to jump-start our day, we'd feel the need to have a living encounter with Him.

The Bible says to taste and see that the Lord is good (Psalm 34:8). Once your soul experiences God in a real and powerful way, you'll crave God more than anything.

Anytime I talk with someone who accepts the Lord, especially those who come to Him late in life, they always lament, "I don't know why I waited so long." Their soul had been starving for God, and they had been feeding on junk food. "As the deer pants for the water brooks, so pants my soul for You, O God" (Ps. 42:1).

Prayer Protection

There's a little red frog in Madagascar called the tomato frog. Whenever it's attacked by another animal, its body leaks out a milky white poison. If the animal tries to eat it, the poison will burn its mouth, and it spits out the frog. The problem is, even though the frog survives, it's all chewed up and hopping around with a limp.

There's no mandate to have your prayer time in the morning, but if you wait until nighttime, you could be like the frog—all chewed up from the day's spiritual battles that you tried to fight on your own.

Imagine how different your day would be if, first thing in the morning, you gave your soul an opportunity to reach up to God. Imagine if, first thing in the morning, you experienced the touch, the assurance, and the wisdom of God. Imagine if, first thing in the morning, you aligned your thoughts, desires, concerns, and fears with the power, reassurance, and faithfulness of God Almighty. And before you faced all the uncertainty of your day, all the lies of the devil and the criticisms of your enemies would be put aside, and you'd be at peace and reassured through your God encounter. Imagine how different your decision-making process would be.

There's Someone bigger and stronger, more faithful than any obstacle you'll ever face. God has created a holy place in your heart for Him to live. It's a place where He wants to meet you every day. I want to encourage you to seek Him there in that place in your heart, and you'll find Him there waiting for you. When you find Him, He'll bless you. When He blesses you, bless someone else.

I
M
A
GOD'S FRIEND
E

Above all of the attributes of our God IMAGE, God created us to live in relationship with Him as His friend. It is within the context of a relationship with God that His love can be experienced and seen in the world. But all too often we seem to prefer living outside of this relationship. God in His love and mercy never gave up on us but pursued us and offers us an opportunity to restore that relationship.

Chapters 13–16 will focus on the "G" component of our God IMAGE and the process of developing a right relationship with God, one through which He can share His love with the world.

13

God's Friend

Relationship

The 2005 movie *The March of the Penguins* is one of my favorite documentaries of all time. It's the story of a colony of emperor penguins that walk seventy miles over twenty days across the frozen continent of Antarctica to the place where they were born. How they can remember where to go, I don't know, but they do. The emperor penguins trek through the harshest weather on earth to their frozen nesting grounds where the females lay their eggs.

After the mother penguin lays the egg, she transfers it to the top of the feet of the dad. If the egg rolls onto the ice, the baby dies. If the transfer is successful, the mom makes the seventy-mile trek back to the sea to fatten herself up with fish to feed her family. During the time she's gone, the dad protects the egg from the ice, sandwiching it between the top of his feet and the bottom of his big belly. There, along with thousands

151

of other dads, he sits for *months* in 120-mile winds, blinding blizzards, and 50-below-zero weather, bringing himself to the brink of starvation and death. If the mom doesn't get eaten herself and makes it back to the dad, and if the chick survives, it has a chance to grow up and one day make the legendary seventy-mile trek itself. But once it gets to the ocean, it jumps into the icy sea and it's gone from the parents forever. This is the part that really gets to me, because after all the parents do for the baby, it will go off on its own to find its own mate and start the cycle all over, never to be seen again by its parents.

I couldn't imagine going through all of that effort to give birth to and nurture my child, only to see it wave good-bye and be gone forever. It broke my heart to think they'd never see their baby again. I cried, and at first did not know why. Then it hit me: I was crying because of my God image.

You and I are the most advanced living creatures God created, and we were created to live in relationships in order to survive. Some animals never see their children. They lay an egg and are gone. The baby comes out of the egg all by itself and is independent at birth. Can you imagine a human baby being independent at birth? Imagine if, after the doctor slaps the baby, it looks at the mom and says, "Hey, Mom, how you doing? Thanks for the womb, and about the hospital bill for the birth, don't worry about it. It's on me." NOT!

The reality is, as humans we are dependent on our parents for decades, and dependent on relationships for life. We can't live without each other. The fourth component of our God IMAGE is the fact that we were created to live in relationship with God as His friend. Created in the image of God, we are hardwired for *relationship*. We long for *connection*. As human beings, we depend on parents or primary caregivers, friendships, and community. The powerful need to develop and maintain relationships is in our DNA.

Our Purpose

The Bible says that God created the oceans and the land, and afterward He said, "Good." God created the trees and plants and He said, "Good." He created the creeping things, the sky, the wind, the clouds, sun, moon, stars, land, animals, fish, birds, and He said it was all *good*. The stars, the sun, and the moon all functioned so perfectly that we can set our clocks by the sun and we can navigate around the world by the stars.

Even though everything God created was good, there was one thing that was not good. In Genesis 2:18 the Lord God said, "It is NOT GOOD that man should be alone." (All you guys, say amen!)

Some of you guys reading this might be thinking, "See? I knew I should have a woman. It says right here in the Bible." When God said that it's not good for man to be alone, He's not talking about males only, but females as well.

But why isn't it good for us to be alone? The answer is directly related to the reason God created humans in the first place. Why do you think God created you? Some people would say that God created humans so they could worship Him, as though God is sitting up in heaven all by Himself craving attention. He loves our worship, of course, and our praise, but God has been receiving worship from angels since long before He created humans. Someone else might say God created humans because He was lonely. Isn't that ridiculous? Not only did He have the angels, but the Father had the Son, the Son had the Spirit, and the Spirit had the Father, and so on. The Trinity had each other and the angels, therefore God was hardly lonely and did not need people.

So why did He create us?

Since God is love and everything He does is based on that love, He lovingly created and designed us to enjoy what He enjoys, which are loving relationships.

Let's think about this for a minute. So many people live life serving the almighty dollar, trying to get paid, buying this and that when they know they don't have the money.

Some people think that if they just get married they will be happy, but marriage doesn't solve that problem. Don't get me wrong, marriage is great, but it is not the source of complete satisfaction.

Then there are others who live by the book, going to church on Sunday, taking care of their garden, saving stray animals, and God says, "Wait a minute. There's more to life than doing good deeds. There's something you're missing; there's something so much *bigger* than your concept of what life is all about."

God lovingly created and designed us to enjoy what He enjoys.

There's certainly nothing wrong with gardens or caring for strays, and certainly nothing wrong with going to church, but God created and designed us for something more important: "I want you to have and enjoy what I enjoy. I want you to fully enjoy *loving relationships* like the ones I enjoy." It is critical that you understand that God just wants to love you.

You don't need to prove anything, earn His love, pay Him back for His love. He just wants you to enjoy His love. If you are living with a burden to prove something, or you are trying to be good enough, don't waste your time. Just receive God's love and live in it.

God is a relationship God. He's been in dynamic, loving relationships since before creation. God the Father, God the Son, and God the Holy Spirit have always been in a relationship called the Trinity.

The Trinity is like a construction project.

Say a construction company wants to build a big mall. First, the owner draws up the plans for the mall. Then he sends his son to sign the contract with the city to build the mall. Then the son sends the general contractor who actually does the work of building the mall.

God, the Father, had the plan of salvation. He sent His Son to sign the salvation contract with His blood, and His Son died and rose from the dead with the promise, "I'm going to send the Holy Spirit to live in My people to bring My plan to completion." Jesus laid the foundation with His life and He continues to build on that foundation through His body, the church.

God is a triune God, three in one, and each has a role. Father, Son, and Holy Spirit, all God, all One, all interacting together with mutual respect and submission, each honoring and loving one another. God sent the Son, Jesus. The Son sent the Holy Spirit. *The Holy Spirit points us to the Son and the Son points us to the Father.* Each member of the Trinity serves and glorifies the other, and they said in Genesis 1:26, "Let Us make man in Our image so We can have a relationship with them."

The love that God expresses in the Trinity relationship is projected onto us as humans in order for us to reflect and emulate loving, mutual, submissive relationships with each other. God's desire is for you to have an intimate relationship with Him, to know Him as He wants to be known, and to live your life as His *friend*.

Friends of God

It might be odd to think of God as a friend, but He himself calls us His friends. Abraham was actually called a "friend of God." Genesis 5:24 says that a man called Enoch "walked with God." Later we meet Moses, to whom God spoke face-to-face as a man speaks with his friend (Num. 12:8).

God uses several labels for us that indicate a close relationship. For instance, the Bible refers to the followers of Christ as His beloved children, His brothers and sisters, His sons and daughters, His sheep, His beloved, His saints, a royal priesthood, a holy nation, His flock, His bride, spouse, chosen, called, elect, and a peculiar treasure. Not only does He refer to us in relationship terms, He has wired our brains and emotions to live in relationship.

Wired for Relationship

Drs. Tim Clinton and Joshua Straub, in their book *God Attachment*, refer to a study made among children as young as three years old who had absolutely no religious or belief system connections. The study discovered that these children possessed a longing or desire for a relationship with a "Transcendent One," meaning one superior and extraordinary, beyond ordinary being: God.

This "God hunger" can be partially explained physiologically by the working of a neurotransmitter in the brain called *dopamine*. The dopamine circuits affect our drive for pleasure, joy, reward, exhilaration, and *seeking meaning to our lives*. Clinton and Straub write, "Research is increasingly making the connection between the dopamine system and one's experience of God."

The authors cite a study tracing the activation of the dopamine system in committed Christians praying the Lord's Prayer. It was concluded that the expectation of the person praying may have been one of receiving back from the prayer *both reward and relationship*.

Scientific studies have discovered that at birth *every* human baby is hardwired to connect with others. *All* scientific research now shows that from the time a baby is born, the brain is already biologically formed to connect in relationships. Experts in children's health publicly recommend that our society pay considerably more attention to young people's moral and spiritual needs.

You're hardwired as a person with a longing for deep, lasting relationships, and the knowledge of a destiny greater than you can create by yourself. That's *God hunger*. It makes complete sense that if God created you to live in relationship with Him, then He also designed you to desire that relationship.

Relationship Rules

While speaking at a men's conference, I asked how many men thought that women were complicated. The room shook as the guys all over the room started yelling and applauding. Then I asked if they knew *why* women were so complicated. The men just sat there.

Well, I figured it out. What I am about to say comes from years of study and interviews with thousands of females. The reason women are complicated is because each female, from birth, has her own specific, unique set of rules on how to love her. Men, when your wife walks into a room with a new outfit, haircut, or earrings, you have a specific amount of time to give a very specific compliment. If you are married, or even in a serious relationship, there are certain other females you are prohibited to talk with, and even with those, not very long. You better bring your wife flowers a specific number of times, and they better be of a specific quality. But this is not what makes females complicated. Females are complicated because they will never, even on your deathbed, tell you what their rules are. You just need to figure them out on your own. That's my own theory.

God, on the other hand, makes it easy for us. He made it clear that to love God is to obey God. Period! The greatest commandment above all commandments is, "You shall love the LORD your God with all your heart, with all your soul, and with all your mind" (Matt. 22:37). Your obedience demonstrates your love for God. "For this is the love of God, that we keep His commandments" (1 John 5:3).

Loving God is obeying God no matter what. It does not matter if you understand why. It does not matter whether you like it or think you will enjoy it or even know precisely how. You just need to do the best you can to do what He says to do when He says do it. That is love for God.

Obedience in Action

When our son Miles was about eleven years old, we caught him lying to his mother. This particular lie was significant, not because of what he said but because of how we dealt with it. I told him that for one solid week he couldn't kiss his mother or tell her he loved her. I also asked my wife not to kiss him or tell him she he loved him. He needed to decide whether to love his mother and not lie, or tell lies and not love her, but he couldn't do both.

To love God is to obey God. To disobey God is to hate God. To be God's friend is to obey God. But if you are going to love and obey God, you will need what Abraham had, for without it, you are doomed.

Faith Hero

Imagine being seventy-five years old and being told by God to leave your family and go to a place that He would show you after you were halfway there. God called Abraham to do just that. He lived in a pagan town with pagan people and didn't know as much about God as *you* do. He was born long before Moses, long before there was a Bible or Ten Commandments. All he had was faith and the promise of God.

God had told him, "I will make of you a great nation, and I will bless you and make your name great, so that you will be a blessing. I will bless those who bless you, and him who dishonors you I will curse, and in you all families of the earth shall be blessed" (Gen. 12:2–3 ESV).

What did Abraham do? He *believed* God.

And just like then, God gives us everything we need to believe Him.

Creatures of Faith

While waiting in the security line at the airport, I started talking to a lady who was on her way to the Philippines. I mentioned I was a pastor. She said she was an atheist. I said, "Really, you don't believe in God?" And she said, "I just don't have any faith."

She couldn't have been more wrong about not having faith. God created us as creatures of faith, and we exercise faith every day, all day. "Faith is the substance of things hoped for, the evidence of things not seen" (Heb. 11:1). We exercise faith every time we turn on the faucet without knowing how water will come out or where it comes from. We have faith every time we turn on the ignition in our car. We may have no idea how something works, but we have faith that the electricity will flow from somewhere through a bunch of circuits and give us the service we want. We have faith that if we jumped off of a ten-story building, then something we have never seen called gravity will pull us down to the ground and we will die. By faith, we stay away from the ledge.

But probably the biggest and most significant step of faith we can take is loving someone. There you are with all your emotions, your expectations of happiness, joy, and companionship, and you hand them to someone, trusting they won't break your heart. Many of us have had our hearts broken. We obviously put our faith in the wrong person, but it was faith nonetheless.

God created us as creatures who must live and love by faith. Regardless of the experiences in our human relationships, we do understand what it means to love by faith, and when it comes time to love God, whom we can't see, we can rest assured that God isn't in the heartbreaking business. He doesn't break hearts; He *mends* them. He has given us plenty of evidence that He exists and loves us, and we can be confident to take the leap of faith in loving Him.

> We fulfill our potential to be the image of God through faith.

You can never say to God that you do not have enough faith to do what God calls you to do, because God will never ask you to do something that He has not equipped you to do. You must know that you absolutely have enough faith to live within a relationship with God and fulfill your potential of the image of God you were created with.

You would think that if you needed a lung transplant, the hospital would do everything to find you one that was a match for your body and when they did, they would give it to you. But not so fast, pumpkin. Besides matching the new lung with your body, they also do an evaluation on your life to ensure that you will take care of the lung. The fact of the matter is, human organs are very valuable and in a lot of cases difficult to come by. As part of their evaluation of your ability to care for the lung, they will check to make sure you can afford the medicine, you will make a commitment not to smoke, and believe it or not, you have a strong community of loving relationships.

One of the most significant indicators of whether you will be alive in ten years is if you are surrounded with close friends who love you. If you do not have a close-knit community of people who love and care for you, you might not get the lung.

We cannot live without relationships, and the most powerful and important relationship is the one we have with God. It will be only in the context of a relationship with God that He will see Himself in and through us as though looking in a mirror.

14

Friendship Breaker

A Satanic Relationship

In a small, crowded church, the preacher is winding down his sermon. The singers are preparing to sing the last song when people start screaming in the back of the church. People are yelling in the lobby, running out of the side doors, and jumping out the windows. The preacher is confused until he realizes what the commotion is all about. The devil has entered the building! Even the pastor starts climbing over the seats and runs out of the church. There's one guy left in the sanctuary, and he's sitting in the front pew casually humming the notes of the last song. The devil stomps up the middle aisle, drenched in slimy nastiness, and he stops in front of the man and growls, "Don't you know who I am?"

The man gives a bored sigh. "Oh yeah, I know who you are. You're Satan."

The devil lets out a roar and the slime flies across the room. "Don't you know what I can do to you? Why aren't you scared of me?"

The man shrugs. "Satan, I've been married to your sister for ten years. You can't do a thing to me that she hasn't already done."

What's the nature of *your* relationship with the devil? That might sound like an odd question, but think about it.

The fourth aspect of our God IMAGE tells us that we're *God's friend*, created to live in a close relationship with Him. Once we become an I AM imposter, we start thinking, "What do I need God for?" Our friendship with God takes a big hit, and our relationship with Satan goes to another level. This chapter will teach us how an I AM imposter identity exploits our need to live in relationship in order to break intimacy and friendship with God. We will also learn the true nature of our relationship with Satan.

Friendship Breaker

Satan speaks three times in the Bible, and in each instance he is trying to accomplish the same thing.

The first time he shows up is in the Garden of Eden as the serpent trying to deceive Adam and Eve and turn them against God. Adam and Eve sinned against God, and as a result they found themselves hiding from God.

The second time is in the book of Job when he tries to turn God against man. Satan approaches God and asks if he might torture Job, claiming that Job was *using* God for the blessings God gave him. He claims that Job would curse God if he lost his riches. God says that Job is the most faithful man around and tells Satan to go ahead and test him. Satan attacks with a fury, and Job loses all ten of his children and everything he owns in a matter of hours. If that wasn't enough, Satan covers his body with painful, oozing boils. Job's wife, in her anguish and confusion, cries out to Job to curse God and die.

Job remained faithful to God and spoke the famous words, "Though He slay me, yet will I trust Him" (13:15). Job's faithfulness and his friendship with God remained intact, and Job had ten more kids and gained more wealth than what Satan destroyed. Job honored God throughout his entire life.

The third time Satan speaks is in Matthew 4:1–11 to taunt the God-man Jesus Himself. Satan tries to get Jesus to worship him instead of God. It didn't work. The number one goal of each of the three conversations is Satan's desire to destroy a relationship with God.

Satan knows that your God image is powerless outside of a dependent relationship with your heavenly Father. Satan clearly knows that you and I were created to grow into a deep and loving relationship with God.

> Satan clearly knows that you and I were created to grow into a deep and loving relationship with God.

Since we were all created to live and flourish in the context of relationship with God, it makes sense that any attack on our God image will result in a broken relationship with God. The actions of an I AM imposter, morality maker, and authority taker will automatically turn you into a *God friendship breaker*.

So what is the nature of your relationship with the devil?

I tweeted this question on Twitter, and I got all kinds of responses. Some of the responses I got to my question were, "I hate Satan." "I have no relationship with him." "He is no friend of mine." "I stay away from him." Unfortunately, all of these people are unaware of the relationship they may actually have with him.

Friend of the World

What is your relationship with the world and the culture in which you live?

The word "world" can apply to the material world. It can also apply to godless living—it's the invisible *spiritual* system of corruption dominated by Satan. This system is in opposition to God, His Word, and His people. Be careful that you haven't become friends with this second definition of "world."

The Bible talks about the dangers of becoming friends with the "world." "Do you not know that friendship with the world is enmity with God?" (James 4:4).

The word "enmity" is a strong one. It means hatred and ill will. If we have a strong emotional attachment to and a deep longing for the vain, selfish things of the world, we not only cloud our relationship with God, we're also taking sides with the one who hates God.

The verse in James goes on to read, "Whoever therefore wants to be a friend of the world makes himself an enemy of God" (v. 4b). An *enemy* of God. If you find yourself criticizing God, arguing with Him, or questioning His judgment, stop right there. These are tell-tale signs of exchanging friendship with God for friendship with the world.

You may not associate these signs with the devil, and that's exactly what he wants you to think: that you have nothing to do with him or that he doesn't exist at all. Know for sure that he's working overtime to take God's place in your life.

What's your relationship with lies or half-truths? When was the last time you said you're late because you got stuck in traffic when there was no traffic? When was the last time you cursed someone out when no one could hear you? When was the last time you engaged in your little secret sins when you thought no one was looking?

Should I mention betrayals, broken promises, degrading yourself, helping yourself to what's not yours? You know in your heart that some of these things are part of your life—some more than others—and since that is true, you and Satan are very involved with each other.

There is no excuse for being casual with the devil. You might not think you have a relationship with the devil because you don't experience a great amount of noticeable evil in your life. (You might not recognize that he's fighting against you because you're already walking with him!) The I AM imposter is someone who tries to sit on the throne where God belongs. When deception takes over, your God image gets so obscured that you become a friend of the world around you, and you forget who you were born to be. You were created to know and love God, to be His image bearer and His *friend*.

It's possible to become so distant from Him that you're not sure if He was ever real. You can get to the point where you have no idea who you are or why you were born. If this is your mentality, God can't operate in and through you as He desires because you have basically turned your back on Him.

You may see glimpses of the good in your life. You can be a person who does good things, a person who recycles, picks up after your dog, does nice things for your mother, brings soup to the sick, studies hard to be a 4.0 student, is kind and capable, works in a helping profession, or gives millions to the poor, but *if your God relationship is broken and your image is blurred, you're lost.*

The real answer to the question about having a relationship with the devil is revealed in the nature of your relationship with God. Is he still God to you, or have you reclassified Him as someone or something else?

Idols

I was at a friend's house one day and couldn't help but notice when he turned toward the wall and said something. I looked at the wall and thought, "Who's he talking to?" It was an idol, a little statue. This guy was talking to a statue!

I see people do all kinds of things they think are spiritual that absolutely baffle me. For instance, you can rub the stomach of a statue all day and night, but it will never bring you luck.

> Their idols are silver and gold,
> The work of men's hands.
> They have mouths, but they do not speak;
> Eyes they have, but they do not see;
> They have ears, but they do not hear;
> Noses they have, but they do not smell;
> They have hands, but they do not handle;
> Feet they have, but they do not walk;
> Nor do they mutter through their throat.
> Those who make them are like them;
> So is everyone who trusts in them.
> Psalm 115:4–8

I AM imposters have not only given themselves a new name and identity, but they have given God a new name and identity. Even though I AM imposters were originally made in the image of God, in their pride they end up returning the favor by remaking God in their own image. They dumb God down to someone who is limited like man and who shows favoritism, makes mistakes, or takes revenge on people. I AM imposters also re-create God in the image of created things, like animals, the stars, or success. Once we do that, we end up worshiping those fake gods or idols as the source of happiness and fulfillment.

Is God a Fool?

A man asked me to pray for him because he had just gotten a DUI. I figured he wanted prayer for God to forgive him for drunk driving.

"Pray God will get me out of it," he said without blinking.

"Get you out of it?"

"Yeah, you know, work a miracle. Get me off. Prove me not guilty."

I looked in his eyes. He wasn't kidding. "But are you guilty?" I asked.

"No. Some guy ran into me."

"That's not what I asked."

He continued to deny what he was responsible for. "If it weren't for that guy who ran into me . . ."

We can be so quick to turn the attention away from the truth, or to blame someone or something else for our mistakes, our problems, and the consequences of our sin. We turn to God in desperate moments, but He's no sucker. He's no fool.

Take a guess what the number one item stolen from our church bookstore is. Bibles! How do you ask God to bless you as you read a stolen Bible? We have the crazy notion that we can dishonor and disobey God and still expect Him to bless us. We think we can live any way we want to live, but He should be ready to jump when we pray. "Do not be deceived, God is not mocked: for whatever a man sows, that he will also reap. For he who sows to his flesh will of the flesh reap corruption, but he who sows to the Spirit will of the Spirit reap everlasting life" (Gal. 6:7–8).

The word "flesh" here doesn't mean just the physical body but refers to ungodly, sinful passions and a devil-inspired selfish nature. God's friends are instructed to deny the flesh. Resist the flesh and acknowledge that our selfish desires only bring drama into our lives.

Is God a Liar?

I was drafted by the Los Angeles Rams in 1982. It was one of the happiest days of my life. This was going to be my first time to Los Angeles. I flew in through Las Vegas, seduction city. From my window seat on the plane, the lights drew nearer as we landed, and then once in the airport, *BAM*—the party was on. Rows and rows of slot machines, lights, stores, restaurants, bars, the glitter, the sparkle, the fun. People go to the Las Vegas strip for a good time, and the airport does a great job of luring you into the city. Satan successfully ruins people's lives because of the false promise he makes about the fun he will give you.

In Luke 4:5–7, the devil took Jesus to a high mountain and said, "I'll give you all the kingdoms of the world if you worship me." He showed Jesus the glitter, the sparkle, the excitement of money and power on earth. He tried to convince Jesus that *he*, not God, had Jesus's best interest in mind. "God lied to you, Jesus, and is holding out on you. I can give you better things than God can." He tried to convince Jesus to settle for any version of wealth, sex, entertainment, and success. "Aw, come on, Jesus, let ME make the choice for you. Let ME be in charge. Let ME take care of things." This is exactly what he whispers in your ear every single day. He wants you to believe that God is to blame for your pain and suffering and that the devil (and the world) has the answer to all of your problems. Unfortunately it's all lies.

Is God to Blame?

A woman who was broken about the pain in her life approached me after church one Sunday. She lost her job, her mom had recently died, and she had some serious health issues. She was just miserable. Before I prayed, she said something that made me take a step back. It sounded like she was blaming God. Wanting to make sure I heard her right, I asked her if she was accusing God of doing something wrong. She said, yes, God had been unfair to her. I don't remember her exact words, but the meaning was clear: she was blaming God for not being fair to her, for allowing her to go through so much pain.

Friendship breakers blame God for war, for world hunger, for disease, accidents, you name it. People ask me all the time, "If God is so loving, why are so many people starving around the world?" Did you know God is probably asking the same thing? He placed more than enough food on the earth to take care of all of our needs. Each year 25 percent, or $450 billion, of the world's food supply is wasted. Is it God who wastes it? NO!

An atheist confronted me with this very argument, claiming that if a loving God really existed, there wouldn't be so much evil and suffering in the world. I explained that God has given man a free will to choose to obey or disobey Him, and the evil and injustice is because man chooses to disobey God. When I AM imposters decide they know more than God, they do more damage than good. The Bible says that there is a way that seems right to man, but in the end it leads to death (Prov. 14:12). The atheist, the ultimate I AM imposter, doesn't understand that people, not God, aren't trustworthy.

Humans misuse His authority and strive mercilessly to control people and nations. Greed and desire for power always mean that suffering results from trying to fulfill that greed. God created everything *good* (Gen. 1:31). Humans commit acts of evil, and then, blinded by pride, arrogantly accuse God of what God had nothing whatsoever to do with.

The Real Father of Lies

One night when I was dating my wife, we were in a club, and I left her alone at the table to go to the men's room. When I came back, another guy was talking to her. I knew this brother was in no way telling her what a great couple she and I made or what a good guy I was. No, he was trying to get her number for himself. Men flatter women for their own sakes, not for the women, just like the devil flatters you for *his* sake, not yours.

The devil knows your weaknesses, knows what you ache for. He'll charm you and tell you anything you want to hear. He's a liar and a flatterer.

God *never* manipulates people with flattery. "Faithful are the wounds of a friend but the kisses of an enemy are deceitful" (Prov. 27:6). God is your friend, and He'll reveal truth to you even if it hurts at times. In the end it will produce righteousness in your life (Heb. 12:11).

> The devil flatters you for his sake, not yours.

Flattery speaks the words your selfish self wants to hear. God speaks the *truth*—He speaks the words your *spirit* needs to hear.

You'll never be loved as deeply and perfectly as God loves you. You'll never be more safe and secure than in His care. You'll never be more YOU than when you are His friend.

Every night when you lay your head on your pillow, someone is going to say, "Well done, good and faithful servant." It will either be God, your true friend, saying things like "Great job setting time aside to pray and read your Bible this morning," or "I really like how you walked away from that gossip conversation that your cousin always tries to drag you into," or "I'm especially proud of you for turning your head away from those half-naked women on your television. Great job today."

But on the other hand, you might hear Satan, your enemy pretending to be your friend, saying things like "Great job tearing down your boss to your co-workers," or "I liked how you yelled and got everyone to watch the television when I flashed those half-naked girls on the screen," or "Carrying your Bible to church on Sunday was good, especially since you and your girlfriend just got out of bed and drove to church in separate cars. You sure have everyone fooled."

Both God and Satan want to be your friend. The choice is yours.

15

Restored Friend of God

Friendship Consultant

I love family reunions. It's fun hanging out, laughing, telling stories about what happened when we were little, and getting reacquainted with grown-ups I remember only as little kids. I like getting to meet all the second and third cousins I never knew I had.

The tables are piled with BBQ'd everything, the music is bumping, and everybody's talking about how good we're all looking, how happy we are to see each other. Relatives talking about what they're up to now, how many operations they've had, who got married, graduated, divorced, died, and what third cousin once removed you never heard of just gave birth to twins who don't look like anybody in the family, not even each other.

There are always one or two people who have the best old pictures of the family. Everyone pulls out their cell phones, wallets, and albums to show their photos. At just about every reunion I meet someone who seems like he just snuck in for the food and isn't actually related to anyone in the family. If there is one thing that I spend most of my time talking about at a reunion is how I'm related to everyone I meet. Can I really trace their family line back to mine?

If Jesus walked up to you today, could you honestly say you were related to Him, and how would you describe that relationship?

Like Friends, Like Brothers

I have two brothers and two sisters whom I love very much. Would I lay down my life for them? *Yes*, but the Bible says "there is a friend who sticks closer than a brother" (Prov. 18:24). There's One closer to you than anyone else, someone who's the most trusting, loyal, loving friend on earth. It's Jesus.

No one in this life will compare with the friendship Jesus offers to you—not your brother, your spouse, your cousin, your mamma, your daddy, *no one*. What's your relationship with Him?

We learned that we were created to be God's friend. We also learned how our blurred image destroys that friendship. This chapter will concentrate on how Jesus can restore or save our relationship with God and how we are to faithfully live in a friendship relationship with Jesus.

There are many titles given to us that imply that we were created to live in a friendship relationship with Jesus. He calls *us* His friends (John 15:15), and we're called brothers and sisters in Mark 3:33–35. But how do we know if we are living as one of His friends?

In the heat of a discussion with someone about salvation, the person asked me, "Isn't there more than one way to get to heaven? You can't really think that Jesus is the only way."

I told him that Jesus asked the same question.

The night Jesus was arrested and then eventually crucified, He prayed in the Garden of Gethsemane with His disciples. He was so stressed over the suffering He was about to endure that the Bible says, "His sweat was as great drops of blood falling down to the ground." He asked the Father if there might be a way out of being crucified (Luke 22:42–44). Basically, He asked what many have asked through the ages: Aren't there other ways to God? Aren't there other ways to get saved?

The Father said to Jesus, "No. Only your death will pay for the sins of the world." Jesus would soon be arrested and crucified, illustrating that His ultimate expression of love as your friend is in laying down His life for you. He explicitly states this in John 15:13: "Greater love has no man than this, than to lay down one's life for his friends." If Jesus died for us, as His friends we must die for others. But what exactly does laying down our lives for our friends mean, and who are our friends?

We've become Jesus's love ambassadors (2 Cor. 5:20), and "laying down our lives" has to mean exactly what it meant to Jesus. The closer our understanding and expression of that phrase matches His, the closer friends we are being. Christ laid down His life for us, and now He wants us to show the people in our lives what that means. He does this *through us*. The ultimate test of our relationship with Jesus is if we allow Him to continue to express His friendship with the world *through us* as He did 2,000 years ago on the cross. The more we sacrifice on behalf of others, the more pure and evident is our friendship with Christ.

Gurrrl

A lady named Susan was very sick and fell into a coma. She was old, and everyone thought she'd die. While in the coma,

Susan saw God, and she told Him, "Oh God, I don't want to die!" and God said to her, "Don't worry. I'll give you eight more years to live."

Susan came out of the coma and was excited that she had eight more years to live, and she could hardly wait to get her groove on. She went out and got a facelift, liposuction, tummy tuck, and shiny white caps for her teeth. She had her hair dyed and permed and a weave, replaced her glasses with contacts. She turned herself into one "hot mommy." As she was shaking and baking her new body across the street into a club, she stepped off the curb, and *BAM*, she got hit by a bus and died. When she woke up in heaven, Susan said to God, "Lord, I thought You said You'd give me eight more years to live!"

God looked at her closely. "Susan?"

She said, "Yeah, it's Susan. I was supposed to have eight more years to live."

He said, "Susan, is that you? Gurrrl, I didn't recognize you!"

The evidence of our friendship with God is our *changed* lives. People with bad attitudes can become the biggest encouragers. Cheapskates can become the biggest givers, and people who are afraid to speak in public can end up as preachers. Do you show evidence of a friendship with God with a transformed life? Can people tell you have been with God? If you are truly a friend, an intimate friend of the Creator of the universe, there is no way that your life cannot change. It is impossible to hang out with a holy God and not be made more and more holy each day.

The greatest evidence of this change is the expression of the most important attribute of God: *Love*. Evidence that you are spending time with God is that you will be sharing and expressing more and more love to the people God brings into your life.

Unconditional Love

A friend of mine had his first child at the age of forty-eight, and he talked nonstop about his experience and his love for that baby. It was his miracle of miracles. Everything the baby did, every sound and movement the baby made, were the most amazing events he'd ever seen. He told me how he would sit up for hours at night and watch the baby sleep. He went on and on about how much he loved her and would do anything for her, even though she did nothing to deserve his love.

We can't earn God's love, and we can't pay Him for favors. God's undeserved favor is called grace. It's His undeserved love. Every blessing He gives us is undeserved. God is so committed to having a loving relationship with us that He created us in His image, and it's as though His heart is living outside Himself and inside of *us*. God loves us freely like my friend loved his baby.

It's easy to show our love to our family and friends, but what about those who don't like us or with whom we don't get along? "If someone says, 'I love God,' and hates his brother, he is a liar; for he who does not love his brother whom he has seen, how can he love God whom he has not seen?" (1 John 4:20).

So how are we to love with God's love?

Two Lines

This is how I think of heaven: As soon as you die, in an instant you will find yourself standing in one of two long lines of people. The people in line number one on the right are partying, laughing, dancing, hugging each other. They're happier and more excited than any people you've seen. Everybody looks good, nobody's cursing, nobody's drunk, everybody's *happy*. You don't know it, but this line is full of people on their way to heaven. The Pearly Gates are sparkling in the distance, the bright lights ahead are glittering, there's sweet music playing, and the people are pumped up.

You can turn and look to line number two. That's the line for hell. Nobody's laughing. You hear crying and groaning. A number of people are fighting. There's no music, no pearly gates in the distance. You can hear weeping and wailing, and ahead there is nothing but blackness punctuated by some orange flames.

Hell is a very real place where those who didn't want anything to do with God on earth go right on eternally having nothing to do with Him. Souls will never see God or anything that resembles Him. In this place there's no goodness because all goodness comes from *God*. There's no love, no loyalty, no friendship, no laughter, and no peace, because all of these come from *God*. Line number two is much longer than line number one. Matthew 7:13 explains that "wide is the gate and broad is the way that leads to destruction, and there are many who go in by it."

> Hell is a very real place where those who didn't want anything to do with God on earth go right on eternally having nothing to do with Him.

While we're alive on earth, the Bible explains that "the rain falls on the just and the unjust"; in other words, God's goodness is everywhere. But not so in hell. Think of this: every human being you know will stand in one of those two lines. God doesn't want anyone to choose line number two, and this is where you and I, Jesus's friends, come in. The most powerful and positive attribute of the people in line number one, those who are on their way to heaven, is *love*.

We're known on earth by our love. In John 13:34–35, Jesus says, "A new commandment I give to you, that you love one another: just as I have loved you, you also are to love one another. By this all people will know that you are my disciples, if you have love for one another" (ESV).

Jesus loves the people in both lines. On earth He was criticized for befriending the people destined for line number two, but He didn't care. Jesus loves *all* people. The Word tells us, "But God demonstrates His own love toward us, in that while we were still sinners, Christ died for us" (Rom. 5:8).

Jesus was a friend of sinners. Luke 11:19 tells us that He was a *friend* of tax collectors and sinners. He hung out with them, and He was willing to take any ridicule and punishment to reach out to them.

> Now it happened, as Jesus sat at the table in the house, that behold, many tax collectors and sinners came and sat down with Him and His disciples. And when the Pharisees saw it, they said to His disciples, "Why does your Teacher eat with tax collectors and sinners?" When Jesus heard that, He said to them, "Those who are well have no need of a physician, but those who are sick. But go and learn what this means: 'I desire mercy and not sacrifice.' For I did not come to call the righteous, but sinners, to repentance." (Matt. 9:10–13)

Jesus's friends reach out to those destined for line number two because those were the very people whom He came to save in the first place. Second Corinthians 5:18–19 says that God has given us the ministry of reconciliation; that is, Christ reconciles the world to Himself, and we've been given the role of ambassadors for Him.

We're God's friends if we do what He does, if we love those He loves, and if we're willing, as Jesus was, to be ridiculed, scorned, and put down for the kingdom of God, because that's what people who are made in God's image do. We live to mirror the loving actions of God. His love does a work in our lives, and then we reach over to the other line of people with the love of God.

Do you hang out with people in line number two, or are you too good for them? Do you want to be seen with them? Do you want to show them love?

Opposites Attract

My wife and I are opposite in almost every way. I talk a lot, and she's relatively quiet. I like working and staying busy, and she's content staying home. I like traveling, and she hates flying. Have you ever wondered why opposites attract?

I have a theory about why God causes two people who are opposites to be attracted to each other. It's His way of placing us in a love relationship that requires self-sacrifice and self-denial. Like all couples, if we're going to get along, my wife and I have to work at denying our own wants to serve each other. Relationships aren't as much about being happy as much as becoming holy, and holiness requires self-sacrifice. Our personal relationships are training grounds for learning how to unselfishly love people. Jesus said that if we are to follow Him, we must deny ourselves, pick up our cross, and follow Him.

Once God's love takes root in us as His friends, His love begins to reach out to those who are far away from Him, like you and I once were.

The Gift of Forgiveness

When I was a youth pastor in San Diego, my wife and I visited the juvenile detention center weekly. I probably visited that place over a hundred times. My wife went with me up until she was eight-and-a-half months pregnant. Those kids were so receptive to the gospel.

One day I got a call about a young man who needed someone to talk to. He had a history of abuse from his dad, and the social worker asked if I'd come and encourage him.

I sat in the cell with him, one-on-one, hoping I could help him. The conversation started with him glaring at me and announcing that he hated black people. After about fifteen minutes of talking, he started cursing me out and yelling at me, calling me the "N word" over and over again.

I eventually walked out, and I could hear him yelling until I was out of the facility. I sat in my car, thinking and praying before driving away. I was not convinced that the boy had anything against me as much as he did against his own life and his pain. That kid needed God desperately, and I believe he wanted God. When he was yelling at me, I didn't take it personally because I could hear his pain crying out for help. In his screams at me I could hear him crying out for his dad to love, accept, and validate him, and to stop hurting him. I heard him crying out for freedom and for someone to be his friend. I also know that while I was in that cell, Jesus was pleading with him through me. This kid was made in the image of God just like you and me, but it was apparent that he lived in an environment with someone who stifled the development of God's image in him.

There are going to be people in your life who will attack you, hate you, and persecute you, but you have to understand that sometimes those actions are code for "I need help," and you must be willing to allow Jesus to love them through you *on Jesus's terms*. If you retaliate and fight back, you'll lose. If you slip back into an I AM imposter mentality, you'll start defending or justifying yourself. No matter what anybody does or says to you, even if they walk up to you and tell you that they hate you, just relax. Their actions have nothing to do with you or who you are. It's all about them, their hang-ups, problems, prejudices, and the lies of Satan. What does Ephesians 6 tell us? We wrestle not against flesh and blood, but against principalities and powers.

Remember, the very people who crucified Jesus were the people He was praying for. Even when they were nailing Jesus to the cross, He prayed for them. He had compassion for His killers. He prayed, "Father, forgive them for they know not what they do." These very words you must—and I mean *must*—stamp permanently into your head. You must, *must*, be ready for every insult, injustice, hateful act, and persecution. You *must* utter silently or out loud, *"Father, forgive them for they know not what they do."*

Being Jesus's friend means being free from carrying injustice and pain on your own shoulders. You're not big enough. The words Jesus spoke on the cross as He died will set you free from bitterness, hurt, anger, shame, and outrage: *Forgive them, Father, for they know not what they do.*

Forgiving is a powerful integrity builder. Being Jesus's friend means not getting in the way of what He wants to do through you in the broken world around you.

Don't act like a fool and fight, but don't shrink back like a coward. Stand tall and maintain your integrity. You are bearing the image of God. Remember, if they persecuted Christ, they will persecute you. The student is not greater than the teacher.

Hatred and the Image Bearer

The experience in the juvenile detention center was a warm-up for what would happen next. This time it would be with a white supremacist incarcerated in an adult men's prison in Southern California. As I was preparing to speak at one of the events out on the yard, God spoke as clearly to me as anyone ever has. He said, "Make sure you tell the men I love them." God was depending on me to bring His love to those inmates. You also have the privilege every day to love the people God brings into your life. Sometimes they are your friends and sometimes they are your enemies, and because God actively loves them, so must you.

An asphalt track circled the yard with a thick orange line alongside the outer edge, which no visitor was supposed to cross. A white dude walked around the track with a couple of other white guys trailing close behind him. All eyes were on this guy strutting around the asphalt track with his chest out. God said, "That's your guy." I walked up to the orange line and waited for him to circle the track next to me, then I called him over.

He paused, looked left and right to see if I was talking to him. He then turned, walked over to me, and looked me up and down. I kept my eyes on him. His jaw was tight, his eyes were narrowed, and he planted himself in front of me with his nose almost touching my nose. His entire body was tattooed with swastikas and white power symbols. What was ironic was that his entire shirtless chest was so covered with white power tattoos that it was almost completely black.

I told him Jesus wanted him.

The other guys in the yard stood watching and waiting for what would happen next. Physically he was making a statement that he was not to be messed with. I stood there with my face up in his face as he glared back at me.

"Yeah," I said, "Jesus wants you."

The more a person promotes himself or herself, the more insecure that person is. Remember, an I AM imposter must spend his life proving and validating his false identity, and one of the ways to do it is by self-promotion. You take someone with insecurity, fear, an oversized ego, someone who is desperate for attention and parental love, and you've got an open door for the devil to take over in that person's life. "Prove yourself, prove yourself," the devil screams into his head, and that person becomes a machine obsessed with self-promotion.

I stood on the orange line looking into two squinty eyes of absolute, total, 100 percent hatred. He gave out a snarling partial laugh and said, "What does *God* want with me?"

Jesus knew people would reject Him, but He loved them anyway. If we go out to minister to others with an agenda in mind, we're missing the point God wants us to make. Sometimes all we're supposed to do is *be there and represent God's love to them*. We leave the results to Him.

When God urges us to love someone, it could be to plant a seed in a heart and not necessarily to see any immediate results at all. God's love is projected on us 24/7, and that love needs to flow *through us or be reflected back out of us 24/7*. Sometimes you'll talk to someone about Jesus, and all you're doing is planting a seed. The person may be someone you know, or it may be someone you'll never see again.

When you stand nose-to-nose with a neo-Nazi racist who not only hates you but hates everyone who looks like you do, what do you do? Jesus didn't put His trust in luck or circumstances or other people. He trusted the Father. One of the ways we can be a friend of God's is to help others establish a relationship with God by dying to ourselves, submitting to Him, picking up our cross, and following Him. You might wonder how you pick up your cross when you are standing on the forbidden orange line in an adult prison yard face-to-face with a racist.

Remember, we are to reflect God's glory in every circumstance, good and bad, nice and not-so-nice. "Christ in you [is] the hope of glory" (Col. 1:27).

God doesn't come and go, sometimes here, sometimes not. If Christ is in you, He definitely wants to pour His love out of you. Is Jesus who the racist saw that day? Better yet, did God feel like He was looking in the mirror at Himself loving that racist that day?

Rejection, accusations, beatings—none of them fazed Jesus when He was on earth. The racist in the prison yard needed Jesus just like you and I did and still do. John 3:16 says, "For God so loved the world that He gave His only begotten Son, that whoever believes in Him should not perish but have everlasting life." God so loved the world, not just the good guys. Here's the difference, though. When God looks at a believer, He sees Jesus in them. When God looks at an unforgiven and unrepentant felon, He sees a blurred image. God's heart is still filled with love for that guy, but there's a difference in what *He sees being reflected back from the felon.*

Just as we know God is with us and helps us when we're in pain, we also recognize pain in the lives of those who reject God. There are people who act out with hate, controlling and manipulating others. Once again, their actions and their words are code for "I need help." We need to look past the offensiveness of outward appearances and behavior to see that they're actually crying out to God.

"What does God want with *me?*" gasped the White Supremacist. "What does *God* want with *me?*"

"He loves you," I said.

He gave a loud snarl, turned on his heel, and continued strutting around the track, showing off his hate tattoos, with his minions following close behind.

Risk or Faith

God's friends, by faith, live the words of Galatians 2:20: "I have been crucified with Christ; it is no longer I who live, but Christ lives in me; and the life which I now live in the flesh I live by faith in the Son of God, who loved me and gave Himself for me." Did the neo-Nazi racist listen to my words that day? I'd like to tell you he heard me and repented on the spot, but that didn't happen. Did that change God's love for him? No. Does it mean I failed? No.

God passionately desires a *relationship* with each of us. He wants us to know Him, enjoy Him, want Him, and love Him. His arms stretch out to us, and He waits for us to enter a relationship with Him that's close, that's *intimate*. God wants us as friends. You may be a distant cousin today, but tomorrow you could be closer than a brother.

16

The Global Church Family

One Body

My family is spread all over the world, from California to New York to Florida to London, so we're hardly ever all in one place at one time. But just before Christmas in 2009, we were finally able to get the whole family together at my sister's in New York, grandkids included. (Needless to say, it was loud in that house.) Before we ate, we stood up around the table, held hands, and I prayed. Just as I said amen, my mother burst out into tears. "This is all I've wanted," she cried. It broke her heart that her family had been scattered and separated for so many years.

I'm sure that it breaks God's heart to see His family, the church, as separated as it is. I'm not saying He wants all of us to be in one physical place at the same time (that's what heaven will be all about), but in order for the church to accomplish God's purpose on the earth, we'll definitely need to be *spiritually in the same place*. When God looks at His church, He wants to see His children working together, getting along, collaborating, partnering, sharing resources, and maximizing the ministry leverage we have as a *family*. He wants to see us collaborating in the same way the Father, Son, and Holy Spirit collaborate.

We know that Jesus performed countless miracles through His ministry on earth. John said that if everything Jesus did on earth could be written down, there wouldn't be enough books in the world to contain it all. In light of this, it seems pretty amazing that Jesus would exclaim in John 14:12 that if we have faith, *we* would do even greater things that *He* did. I wonder how many people actually believe it. It's a powerful statement about the potential of the church. Jesus knew we'd collectively be able to love more people, feed more people, heal more people, and encourage more people than He did during His ministry on earth. If the church would work together as one family, led by the Holy Spirit, there's no limit to what we could do.

> If the church would work together as one family, led by the Holy Spirit, there's no limit to what we could do.

If we're going to live in relationship with God as His friend, we must also live in relationship with His family, the global church. In this chapter we'll focus not only on the ways that God would have us live and operate in relationship with our extended global church family but also on the powerful benefits that relationship would bring to the world.

First we must acknowledge our connection with the global church. During a citywide prayer meeting of about 5,000 believers from dozens of churches, a pastor walked up to the microphone and asked everyone in the crowd, on the count of three, to shout out the name of their church. When they did, all you could hear was screaming babble.

We all started laughing and thought to ourselves, what was the point of that? For one, our being there together was an expression of our desire to be unified and this seemed to highlight our differences. Second, we couldn't understand one word anyone said.

But he wasn't done with his illustration. He then said, "On the count of three, everyone shout out the name of your Lord."

A buzz went through the crowd and everyone sat straight up in their seats.

We got it. We now knew where he was going and it was really good.

He shouted, "One, two, three," and everyone screamed, "Jesus!"

You could hear the excitement and the desire to be one, united church and immediately we knew the power that came with that unity.

The speaker said that even though there are over 1,100 congregations that meet on Sunday mornings in San Diego, there is only one church, and we need to begin acting like it. This principle applies to every believer in the world.

Matthew 12 tells the story of Jesus teaching a Bible study when His mother and brothers arrived to see Him, but they couldn't reach Him through the crowds of people. When Jesus is told His mother and brothers are standing outside wanting to speak to Him, He looked out at the crowd in the house and told them, "Here are My mother and My brothers! For whoever does the will of My Father in heaven is My brother and sister and mother" (vv. 49–50).

You have spiritual brothers and sisters in every country of the world, but do you care to know about the spiritual battle they might be going through or the spiritual needs they may have that you can help meet? Are you concerned about your brothers and sisters who are suffering and being killed for their faith? Do you care? I'm not saying you need to know everything about the millions of believers around the world and do something to help all of them. Still, we're given a global mandate as part of the global church to make new disciples and care about the world as God does. Every Christian in the world is your relative.

> Every Christian in the world is your relative.

So how can we live and work together to fulfill God's purposes? How can we love and care for each other better as family? When the church is disconnected, we're weak and at a collective disadvantage. When we find out that one part of the church hurts, we should all hurt. When the church is attacked, the bullets are aimed at each of us.

Think about it this way: if God created us in His image so He would live in and through us, consequently seeing Himself in us as looking in a mirror, then whatever breaks His heart needs to break our heart.

There are people suffering right now for their faith, and we need to get in touch with their pain and stop living in Christian fantasyland. There are those whose trials are severe, and they need us.

The following is a compilation of reports from websites tracking religious persecution.

> Murderous rioting sparked by Muslim attacks on Christians and their property in Jos, Nigeria, on November 28–29, 2010, left six pastors dead, at least 500 other people killed, and 40 churches destroyed. Nigerian church leaders counted more than 25,000 people displaced in the two days of brutality. What began as outrage over suspected vote fraud in local

elections quickly hit the religious fault line as angry Muslims took aim at Christian sites rather than at political targets. Police and troops reportedly killed about 400 rampaging Muslims in an effort to quell the unrest, and Islamists shot, slashed or stabbed to death more than 100 Christians.

And look at what's happening to our family in Somalia. At least 24 foreign aid workers were murdered there last year. One was beheaded for converting from Islam to Christianity. Muslim extremists from the al Shabaab group fighting the transitional government sliced the head off 25-year-old Mansuur Mohammed, a humanitarian aid worker, before horrified onlookers of Manyafulka village, 10 kilometers (six miles) from Baidoa.

In many parts of the world Christians are afraid to admit their faith. A 40-year-old mother of ten children was fetching firewood with her 23-year-old pregnant daughter, Asha Ibrahim Abdalla, in Yontoy when a group from al Shabaab approached them and asked if they were Christians. "We openly said that we were Christians," the mother said. "They began beating us. My son, who was ten years old, escaped and ran away screaming. My daughter was six months pregnant and crying. They hit me at the ribs before dragging both of us into the bush. They raped us repeatedly and held us captive for five days." The Muslim extremists left them there to die, she said. Found by her husband, Bilal, the beaten and nearly incoherent mother and daughter were taken to the Dadaab refugee camp where the daughter, Asha, prematurely gave birth to a very sick baby. Such cruel and sadistic attacks on innocent people are not uncommon in Somalia.

You're probably thinking that you need to pray more for your brothers and sisters, and asking yourself how you can help them. Maybe you're thinking, "I'm glad these atrocities aren't happening where I live," but one of the reasons for sharing these stories with you is so you'll see the amazing courage of your family and be challenged to take a stronger stand for Jesus yourself. These brave lives should force you to question what intimidates you and keeps you from courageously sharing your faith.

Too many of us are afraid to share our faith with our family, neighbors, and community, but why? What reward is there in fearful silence? How pitiful is it to be afraid of verbal criticism when our brother and sisters are being murdered for speaking out about their faith? How sad that we so quickly back down from defending our faith in Jesus out of fear of ridicule when our brothers and sisters are being mutilated and beheaded for defending their Christian faith.

During my second year with the San Diego Chargers, we were playing the Denver Broncos, and John Elway threw a pass to the right end that I was covering. When I dove to intercept his pass, I landed on my elbow. The force of the fall snapped my collarbone. I got up and walked about the field thinking my shoulder was hanging kinda funny. I was taken to the locker room, and in order to be examined, I had to lift my arm straight up to get my shoulder pads off, which nearly killed me. The x-rays showed my collarbone was snapped in half.

A week later I stood on the sideline and thought how my legs were in shape, my mind was in shape, I knew all the plays, and I could run all day. Countless functions must occur simultaneously for our bodies to operate. My body was strong, but because of one bone, the rest of my body couldn't play football.

Just as with the physical body, the body of Christ can't function to its full potential unless each of the parts works with the others to fulfill their tasks. The body of Christ is a global body or family, and there are some parts that function very well while other parts are under-funded or under-resourced or going through persecution and not functioning well at all. The body of Christ needs to work to strengthen the parts that are lacking or hurting. If there are parts of the body that can't function properly, they're preventing the whole body, the whole family of God, from accomplishing everything God designed for us to accomplish. We *must* have a global picture. The unique needs of our global family provide ministry opportunities for all of us, no matter where we live.

World Ministries

There are countless ministries serving the needs of our global family and giving people opportunities to serve the world. The need for clean water, food, medical care, and decent living conditions are great in many parts of the world. According to a study made by the World Hunger Education Service (http://www.worldhunger.org), the number of hungry people in the world reached 925,000,000 in the year 2010. These statistics are staggering. Here are just three ministries reaching out with helping hands:

> **Heifer International**: This humanitarian organization sends livestock to people in disadvantaged countries in order to help them out of poverty. Providing training along with the gifts of livestock, they help families generate income through their own efforts and also improve their nutrition. In exchange for their livestock and training, families agree to give one of their animal's offspring to another family in need. It's called "Passing on the Gift"—a cornerstone of the mission to create an ever-expanding network of hope and peace. Heifer International currently provides twenty-eight types of animals to families in need in more than fifty countries, including the United States. Their credo: "By giving families a hand-up, not just a hand-out, we empower them

to turn lives of hunger and poverty into self-reliance and hope."

Hydromissions International: This Christian ministry provides clean water wells all around the world to supply people with clean sources of water. One out of five deaths of children under five years old is a water-related issue. Nearly one billion people lack a good clean source of water.

World Vision: This well-known international ministry works in over a hundred countries in the world. They provide loans to women so that they can start a business to feed their family. They provide disaster relief and sponsorship of desperate children. Founded in 1950, World Vision serves close to one hundred million people around the world regardless of religion, race, ethnicity, or gender in times of earthquakes and hurricanes, famine, and civil war. They provide aid and help for refugees and survivors, abandoned and exploited children, and families in communities devastated by AIDS in Africa, Asia, and Latin America. They don't hesitate to go where the need is greatest. Their website is: http://www.worldvision.org.

You might still be asking yourself what you could possibly do. These ministries are reaching out to your brothers and sisters around the world, and you can be a part. The opportunities are out there for you to make a difference.

The first thing you can do is get informed. The internet can bring you right into the lives of your global family, and prayer can bring your family into the presence of God. Someone once told me that we become intimate with the God we pray *to*, the people we pray *with*, and whomever we pray *for*. Start praying for your family on the other side of the world and watch what God does.

Global Starts at Home

The global church includes those who are living in our very own communities.

Imagine if each believer had the courage to stand up for the gospel in his or her own hometown. Imagine if we were willing to go help the lost single person living in the apartment right next to us. Imagine how powerful the church would be if we began to acknowledge the other parts of our body who are suffering, hiding, and discouraged.

There are plenty of family members living down the street from you or in your own home who need your love and encouragement. Let me encourage you to ask God to use you and give you an outlet to nurture a better relationship with your spiritual family at home and around the world.

I
M
A
G

PART 5

ETERNAL

As God is eternal, so we are eternal. Unfortunately there is an eternal battle for our souls—a battle that many are losing. All too often we get too caught up in the here and now.

Chapters 17–20 will focus on the "E" component of our IMAGE to help us develop an eternal focus for our lives and develop an eternal plan for our souls.

17

Eternal Being

You Will Never Die

Whenever I officiate a funeral, one of the first questions I ask about the person who died is, "Did they have faith in God?"

I realize that the family members want the answer to be as close to yes as possible. The answers I get are all over the place. Some say the person did believe but didn't go to church, or "No, she didn't talk much about God, but I know she believed in God." Others say, "He wasn't much of a churchgoer, but he treated people the way they wanted to be treated, lived the golden rule, and never hurt anyone," or "She was the kindest person I ever met. Better than any Christian I know." Everyone is wondering, where is this person now? No one wants to admit that the deceased denied God but still expects to be in heaven for eternity with Him.

The concept of eternity is a universal belief, but why? It is because eternity is *in* you, in all of us. Ecclesiastes 3:11 says that He has made everything beautiful in its time, and He has put eternity into your heart. Eternity is in us because God put it there. We will spend eternity somewhere.

> You are going to live forever somewhere.

Nobody is created to live and then vanish into nothing. You are going to live forever *somewhere*. There's eternity in every one of us; we have an inborn knowledge and *longing* for the eternal. The fifth and final aspect of our God IMAGE is the fact that we were uniquely created as eternal beings designed to have an eternal relationship with God.

Eternal God

God is eternal, the I AM. He has no beginning and no end. The Bible claims that God existed before time because He existed before the beginning. Genesis 1:1 says, "In the beginning God . . ."

The last book of the Bible also claims that God will exist after what we know as reality is destroyed. He exists independently and eternally. "'I am the Alpha and the Omega, the Beginning and the End,' says the Lord, 'who is and who was and who is to come, the Almighty'" (Rev. 1:8).

Spirits are eternal, and God is Spirit. He formed us as eternal spirit beings and gave us a temporary human experience, according to Zechariah 12:1: "Thus says the LORD, who stretches out the heavens, lays the foundation of the earth, and forms the spirit of man within him."

It is the spirit in us that gives us life.

I was in Edmonton speaking for a youth conference and decided to go for a jog before I went to the arena. As I ran into the park, I saw a few police cars near the entrance and about five officers standing on the grass around a dead body.

Other than at a funeral or in anatomy class, I had never seen a recently deceased body. It didn't look like someone sleeping but more like someone frozen.

The lifelessness of the body shows that it is void of energy. When God created man, He breathed the breath of life in him, a life-giving force that guides our actions, dreams, and aspirations and gives us glimpses into the unseen eternity. This unseen spirit is not limited by the limits of our physical bodies. It came from God and is destined to return to God. It is eternal.

Spirits do not die in the sense that we understand death for our physical bodies. Even though the Bible talks about people being spiritually dead, a dead spirit is not one that ceases to function but a spirit that is not able to respond and please God.

If God is spirit and eternal, and we are created as spirit and eternal, what about heaven? How often do you find yourself thinking about where you will go when you die? If you believe there is an afterlife, you are right. You are going to spend a lot more time in eternity than you will on this life on earth, so it is critical that you get this right.

Heaven Is Real

Referred to over 600 times in the Bible, heaven is the eternal destination for God's people. Heaven is where Jesus promised to go and prepare a place for us. John 14:1–4 says,

> Let not your heart be troubled; you believe in God, believe also in Me. In my Father's house are many mansions; if it were not so, I would have told you. I go to prepare a place for you. And if I go and prepare a place for you, I will come again and will receive you to Myself; that where I am, there you may be also. And where I go you know, and the way you know.

There's no anger, no frustration, no bitterness, and no anxiety in heaven. Revelation 21:4 tells us that in heaven "God will wipe away every tear."

After Jesus made promises to prepare a place for us in heaven, He ascended to heaven. But it gets better than that. The Bible also tells us that Jesus will descend from heaven to receive us to Him.

> For the Lord himself will descend from heaven with a cry of command, with the voice of an archangel, and with the sound of the trumpet of God. And the dead in Christ will rise first. Then we who are alive, who are left, will be caught up together with them in the clouds to meet the Lord in the air, and so we will always be with the Lord. Therefore encourage one another with these words. (1 Thess. 4:16–18 ESV)

The Afterlife

Have you had the experience where you look at your life and groan, "Is this all there is?" Your eternal spirit is yearning for something more, because your eternal nature can conceive that there is something more to yearn for.

I'm here to tell you that *no*, this is *not* all there is. Inside your heart of hearts you know that. You're wired to know that. The eternal aspect of your God image seeks God and the eternal reality He has created for you to experience. We can't help but be concerned about where our loved ones are after they've left the earth. We can't help wondering about our own afterlife. God has given us the ability to imagine and desire eternity and an eternal place.

One of the characteristics of being eternal is experiencing it now. Since eternity is forever, it has already begun. You are already experiencing it; therefore it is already having an impact on your thinking and interests.

Reaching for Eternity

There was a little boy walking in the park with a soap bubble blower thingee. You know, the little plastic bottle full of soapy water and a plastic stick with a ring on the end. You stick the plastic ring into the soapy water, take it out, and blow bubbles up into the air. Well, this little boy was in a park, walking in circles and looking up into the sky as he blew bubble after bubble.

Then all of a sudden a huge bubble began floating down from the sky. He stood there with his eyes and mouth wide open as the red bubble dropped and popped on top of him. It made him smile. No, really, a make-you-smile good feeling washed over him. He rushed to put his stick into the soapy water and blew another bubble up into the sky, and two more huge bubbles, this time blue and purple, fell out of the sky and popped on him again. Each time he sent a bubble into the sky, two or three more bubbles dropped and popped on him.

But the bubbles from the sky were no ordinary bubbles. They not only dropped and popped, they spoke to him. They encouraged him in times when he was discouraged. They gave him wisdom in how to deal with peer pressure at school. They gave him vision on the direction of his life, even at his young age. The more the sky bubbles fell on him, the stronger his desire to have them fall on him became.

Like the boy blowing those bubbles, when you pray, you are reaching into the unseen eternal world. Prayer is communication with an eternal God. The answer to that prayer is what makes prayer real. Without an answer, prayer is futile.

Don't get me wrong, when I say answer, I am not saying that you get what you ask for. Any response to your prayer is an answer. It may not be the answer you were looking for because prayer is not about you getting what you want. It is about God getting what He wants. You are reaching out to an eternal, all-knowing, all-powerful God for insight, wisdom, and strength that you do not have to do things you cannot do.

This interaction called prayer can only happen if the eternal aspect of who you are can cry out to and connect with an eternal God. God created us as eternal spiritual beings so we could communicate and have a relationship with an eternal spiritual God.

Because our God image is eternal, people all over the world from generations past have been attempting to connect with an eternal being. Religions of every culture, nation, and time have made a cult of death and the afterlife. From the ascetic monk in his desert cave to the heathen pharaoh on his golden throne, eternity and the afterlife have been a major aspect of religious thought.

18

Temple of Doom

Death

In the movie *Zombies*, dead people come back to life and try to turn others into zombies. The dead people, or zombies, appear to be alive but are, in fact, *dead*. They walk around, make sounds, move their arms and legs, but they're *dead*.

Spiritually dead people are very similar. They serve their community, they drive cars, they have nice clothes, they speak well, but they're spiritually dead. They're dead. Spiritually dead people breathe, go to work, and make money, but they abuse their authority by making their own moral rules. They live like I AM imposters without God as their anchor, and then one day they die like everyone else. But existence doesn't end at the funeral. We're spirit beings, and our spirits don't die. We exist somewhere forever.

Material things and our bodies don't live forever, but our *spirits* live forever. God created our bodies to be His temple, a dwelling for His Spirit to live. "Do you not know that your body is the temple of the Holy Spirit who is in you, whom you have from God, and you are not your own?" (1 Cor. 6:19).

We've already learned that we are eternal beings, and when we live consistent with our God image, heaven awaits us. We learned that God created us to live in a relationship with Him for all eternity. The I AM imposter, who is also an eternal being, often discovers too late that the body, instead of being the temple of God, has become the Temple of Doom.

> You were not created to die. You were created to live forever. Where will your forever be?

God breathed His eternal breath into all humans. His breath is *spirit*. We are created body, soul, and *spirit*. Our bodies will one day die, but our spirits live forever. Our task on earth is to live in *spiritual oneness* with God. Death doesn't release us from the consequences associated with rejecting God. Since rejecting God is a spiritual offense, and we're eternal spiritual beings, the consequences for that rejection must be spiritually eternal.

This chapter is going to cover what happens eternally when our God image lives in opposition to God. What's the inevitable eternal destination for the I AM imposter?

You were not created to die.

You were created to live forever.

Where will your forever be?

Hell on Earth

When you look at the evil in the world, please understand that, as the instigator, the devil is behind every bit of it. War, pestilence, disease, murder, rape, poverty, hunger—all of it is instigated by the devil. What kind of a place would be a just punishment for the instigator of every evil thing ever done on the earth? God calls it Hell, *Gehenna* and *Tartarus* (Greek), *Hades* and *Sheol* (Hebrew), Bottomless Pit, the abode of the Dead, the Place of Punishment, Lake of Fire, Outer Darkness, Furnace of Fire, Everlasting Contempt, Fate of the Wicked, Chains of Darkness.

Heaven is a place of joy and beauty and goodness, of peace and bliss, where sickness and tears are no more, where there is joy everlasting. Hell is a place of torment, of weeping and gnashing of teeth. Hell is the place where every good thing associated with God is absent. It's a terrible place that God originally designed to bring justice to Satan and his demons. "Then he will say to those on his left, 'Depart from me, you cursed, into the eternal fire prepared for the devil and his angels'" (Matt. 25:41 ESV). Hell wasn't originally intended for humans. It's critical to keep in mind that heaven was our destiny until we decided to reject God and have a relationship with Satan. Living for or against God, consistent or inconsistent with God's image, is a *choice*.

Heaven rewards God's faithful image bearers. Great joy waits for those faithful ones who sacrifice the temporary pleasures in this world for the everlasting joy of heaven.

Eternal Choice

Whenever I travel internationally, it's always a relief to cross the border back into the United States of America. I love talking to the customs agents, especially if they're from New York, my home state. Crossing that border reminds me of how proud and happy I am to live here. I have absolutely no desire to live anywhere else, and it would be unfair for anyone to force me to become a citizen of another country. People who deny God all their lives send a clear message to Him that they don't want to be citizens of heaven. It would be unfair and even unloving for God to *force* heaven on them. Another word for forced intimacy is rape, and God has no intention of committing spiritual rape on anyone.

We must choose to love God.

During my first two years in professional football, I used cocaine, smoked marijuana, was sexually immoral, you name it, and I did it all with my partner in crime, my main man, Danny. We did just about everything together. When I gave my life to Christ and gave up that lifestyle, he continued right on partying. One day while driving in the car, I turned to him and asked him about his interest in the Lord. He turned toward me and said something that I'll never forget. He told me, "Miles, if it weren't for people like me, you wouldn't have a job." In other words, he was telling me that if he and other sinners started going to church, there would be no sinners for me to witness to. What hurt the most was, he was also telling me that he had decided to reject God and live for himself.

Suppose that even though God was loving Danny, he just continued to turn his back and go his own way without God? If Danny denied Him all his life, why would God *force* him to live forever in heaven in a close relationship with Him? Danny had made it clear that he wasn't interested. (I am so glad to say that Danny has since walked away from this mind-set.)

It's a logical conclusion that if you're a spiritual being living consistent with God's plan for your life, you'll spend eternity in heaven with Him. But if you're pushing Him away all your life, wouldn't it be fair to you to continue on eternally without Him? Why would God go against your wishes and force you to join Him in heaven when you spent your entire life telling Him you don't trust Him, don't believe in Him, and don't want Him or His Word involved in your life?

If you were to die and stand before God today and the only evidence of your worthiness to heaven was your actions toward the things of God, would you get into heaven? In other words, what message have your actions sent to God and the world?

Hell for Dummies

Hell is the place God has set apart for the devil and his demons, and those who reject God get to join their demon cohorts in hell forever. The murderer who dies cursing God will be met by the ringleader of that curse, Satan himself, and he'll meet a fate far worse than those he murdered. "For the wrath of God is revealed from heaven against all ungodliness and unrighteousness of men, who suppress the truth in unrighteousness" (Rom. 1:18).

Jesus actually calls Satan their father.

> You are of your father the devil, and the desires of your father you want to do. He was a murderer from the beginning, and does not stand in the truth, because there is no truth in him. When he speaks a lie, he speaks from his own resources, for he is a liar and the father of it. But because I tell you the truth you do not believe Me. (John 8:44–45).

If there were a book called *Hell for Dummies*, here's how it would begin: "God didn't create dummies, and He didn't create you to spend eternity in hell (Matt. 25:41). You were created to live with God forever. Self-made dummies have choices like everybody else."

Hell Warnings

I remember my first hangover. I was in high school. I do not remember everything that I drank except the last thing that I almost threw up. It was a 40-ounce bottle of Colt 45. I remember rolling out of my friend's car, barely walking home (and I lived next door). That night and the next morning felt like everything I imagined about hell. That hangover was a warning of what to never do again.

God lovingly gives us constant warnings to remind us of the hell to come. He consistently reveals to us the death and pain that's associated with rejecting God. These warnings foreshadow the compounded pain waiting in a place where there'll be no remnant of the good that God represents. I want you to think of the worst screams you've ever heard and put them in an imaginary bottle. Then think of the worst physical pain, mental or emotional stress, or spiritual oppression you've ever experienced and put it in the bottle. Now, shake up the bottle and drink it. *That's* a taste of *hell*. If you've ever been depressed, suicidal, lonely, or empty, you've had a small taste of hell. If you've ever just sat alone and hurt, you've had a small taste of hell.

But conversely, anywhere there's love, joy, peace, patience, kindness, joy, confidence, hope, that's a taste of *heaven*. Anywhere God has control of everything is a taste of heaven. And when God leaves the scene, the only thing left is hell, because hell is separation from Him. We learn day after day that we reap what we sow, yet we continue to be with people who hurt us, we get drunk only to suffer hangovers, break the law only to go to prison. Proverbs 26:11 says, "As a dog returns to his own vomit, so a fool repeats his folly." Vomit tastes nasty, so why keep eating it?

I was speaker at a youth conference in northern California, and at the end of the session I opened it up to questions from the audience. A young man stood up and asked, "Suppose I lived my whole life getting high, partying, doing bad stuff, and right before I die, I repent and ask Jesus to forgive me. Will I go to heaven?"

I said, "Sure, if you are sincere." God is a forgiving God, and it's a big deal to Him when a person repents and surrenders to Him, no matter when.

The boy said, "Why would God let me cheat Him like that?"

I said, "No, the person getting cheated is you. You've missed out on the blessings of the abundant life Christ offers now, in this life."

He frowned. "But it was a great time!"

"Not as great as it would have been with the Lord," I told him. "So really, you're the one who got cheated on the deal."

Think about it, after you've had some of Satan's so-called fun, you gotta go to the clinic, you end up in jail or drug rehab, you're beat up, broke, uneducated, hospitalized, maybe even homeless. Satan's "fun" will have you waking up in the morning next to someone you don't know, hating your parents, or wanting to kill yourself.

God gives us warning after warning and tells each of us, "I love you, and want to be with you as your friend on earth and forever in heaven." You know there is eternity, and you know God has evidence that He warned you where not to go and what not to do, including through this book you are now reading. Let me encourage you to take a good look at the evidence and know that God, the judge, will not be found wrong in the final court case for your soul.

More Than Fair

I was talking to a guy who was complaining about not getting a job. He said that God was not fair. I agreed with him. God is not fair; He is righteous. Think about it. God projects His love and creativity on people who don't give Him credit for their ideas. God projects His patience on those who stay angry at the world and everyone in it. God projects His kindness on people who are cruel to others. God projects his unconditional love on those who hate Him.

In Matthew 5:45 Jesus says, "[God] makes His sun rise on the evil and on the good, and sends rain on the just and on the unjust." If God were fair, He would've had all of us pay the price for our own sin a long time ago. It would be fair for God to punish those who, in their actions and words, curse His name day and night.

But happily, God is not fair. No, God is *merciful* because He doesn't give us what we deserve. God is *gracious* because He gives us what we don't deserve, which is another chance to repent and tell Him we love and appreciate the abundant and eternal life He offers us. God is *righteous* because in the end He will judge according to His eternal justice.

First John 4:16 says *God is love*. You were created to know God's love and live in His glorious presence all your life. You were created to spend eternity with Him. You weren't created to be a Temple of Doom but the temple of God and fulfill the potential of God's image.

19

Restored for Eternity

Eternity Consultant

A friend of mine walked into a company for what would seem like a routine job interview, but he was sweating bullets. As a teenager, he committed a crime and was concerned that it would come back to haunt him. But because he committed the crime as a juvenile, when he became an adult, his criminal record was "sealed." Sealed means the crime is no longer on his record and publicly accessible. It's like he never committed the crime. When he goes for job interviews, he doesn't have to mention his police record because it's as good as gone. But even though his record was sealed, it didn't erase from his mind the possibility of it somehow interfering with his employment.

It's logical to think that once God forgives us of our sins, they're "sealed," and all we need to do is live the rest of our life walking with God, and one day we'll die and go straight to heaven. After all, the Bible tells us, "If we confess our sins, He is faithful and just to forgive us our sins and to cleanse us from all unrighteousness" (1 John 1:9). That's good news! Those confessed sins are gone from our records. "I, even I, am He who blots out your transgressions for My own sake; And I will not remember your sins" (Isa. 43:25).

When you repent and ask for forgiveness, Jesus absolutely forgives you. Unfortunately, even though you've been forgiven, before you enter into eternity you'll still face a *judgment*. It'll be a different kind of judgment day than those going to hell will face, but it's judgment just the same. Judgment determines the experience you will have in heaven, and Jesus is the One who prepares you for that individual heaven experience. We won't all have the same heaven experience. That's right, your experience in heaven will be different than mine. Don't get me wrong; we will both be having a great time, but it will be unique and different. Therefore, we need our own individual prep for it.

In this chapter, we'll focus on the role Jesus has in the final preparation for eternity for believers. His residency in our hearts ensures that when God the Father looks at us, He sees Himself, as if He were looking in a mirror. Therefore when we die, Jesus has one more assignment to prepare us for before we enter into eternity.

Judgment Belongs to Jesus

When you face God on that great day, you'll be looking into the loving, forgiving face of Jesus. "For the Father judges no one, but has committed all judgment to the Son, that all should honor the Son just as they honor the Father. He who does not honor the Son does not honor the Father who sent Him" (John 5:22).

Jesus will judge believers as well as nonbelievers. We learned in the last chapter that nonbelievers will be judged and sent into eternity away from God. But Jesus will also judge believers from what is called, in Greek, a *bema*, a "high place," a platform or step. The word *bema* is also used for "judgment seat." In front of the *bema*, or judgment seat of Christ, is where we'll find ourselves standing at our final moment of preparation for eternity.

Are you living your life as someone who is preparing for the test that Jesus will put you through when you die? Or are you just cruising, thinking that God's grace is going to take care of everything for you?

Eternal Jesus

My sister and I recently visited my parents' house and started looking at old family pictures. Because there were five kids all born within a six-year period, it seemed like there was always one of us with our hair all jacked up. Mom was really busy, and we were some crusty kids growing up. There were pictures of our first day of school, football pictures, playing in the pool, vacation shots, Christmas, birthdays, graduations, and hanging out at home. If I didn't find any pictures of *me* in all of our family photos, it would be hard to believe I was actually there, wouldn't it? If Jesus is really God and really *eternal*, you'd expect to find Him in the Old Testament as well as the New Testament. In God's family album, the Bible, Jesus is present as far back as *before* creation!

In Jesus's prayer recorded in John 17, He prayed, "And now, Father, glorify me in your presence with the glory *I had with you before the world began*" (v. 5 NIV). Colossians 1:15–16 says, "He [Jesus] is the image of the invisible God, the firstborn over all creation. For by Him all things were created that are in heaven and that are on earth, visible and invisible, whether thrones or dominions or principalities or powers. All things were created through Him and for Him." John 8:58 says, "Jesus said to them, 'Most assuredly, I say to you, before Abraham was, I AM.'"

These biblical pictures of Jesus affirm an eternal Jesus. We are created *in His image* to live in relationship with Him forever. Right now we're living on earth, and God has given us a clear picture of what our eternal relationship with Jesus looks like. It's this eternal Jesus who not only *grants* us eternal life, He also *prepares* us for eternal life.

The Test

Jesus will expose you—your words, thoughts, and actions, and the intent of your heart during your life—to His judgment fire. The fire exposes the level of faith you exercised while on earth. Everything you've accomplished by faith in Jesus survives the fire and is eligible for a heavenly reward. Anything not done by faith in God—whether done out of selfishness, pride, fear, or whatever—will not be eligible for a heavenly reward and will be burned in the fire. The fire of God is a refining process, meant to reveal how well you lived by faith and determine your heavenly rewards, which will ultimately determine your heaven experience.

Glory Bling

When I got engaged, the first thing I needed to do was get a diamond, and I knew nothing about them. I soon learned that the value of a diamond is determined by the diamond's ability to reflect light.

When I bought the diamond for my wife's engagement ring, she kept holding it up to the light to show off its bling. Diamonds bling or sparkle only if light shines onto them. A diamond takes plain white light and magnifies it, splitting it up into many colors. The heavenly rewards or crowns we receive in heaven are designed to reflect God's glory back to Him in the most pure and powerful way.

Jesus sits on the throne of heaven forever and ever. Look what it says in Revelation 4:9–11:

> Whenever the living creatures give glory, honor and thanks to Him who sits on the throne, who lives forever and ever, the twenty-four elders fall down before Him who sits on the throne and worship Him who lives forever and ever, and cast their crowns before the throne, saying:
>
> "You are worthy, O Lord,
> To receive glory and honor and power;
> For You created all things,
> And by Your will they exist and were created."

These verses tell us that we'll fall down and worship Him; we'll lay our crowns before the throne and cry out, "You are worthy O Lord, to receive glory and honor and power, for You created all things, and by Your will they were created and have their being!" We glorify God through our sacrifice, our surrender, and our worship. Evidence of this is exactly what the fire is looking for in the refining process.

> We glorify God through our sacrifice, our surrender, and our worship.

Fingerprint Evidence

When crime scene investigators go out to investigate a crime scene, they look for evidence of who did what. They look for DNA evidence, bodily fluids, footprints, tire prints, and fingerprints. Fingerprints tell them who touched what. When we stand before God, He's looking for fingerprint evidence. He's going to look for *His* fingerprints on us and our life.

How many of your own fingerprints are on your life compared to God's fingerprints? Is your life about what you do, or is it about what God and only God can do? How many times have you said to yourself, "This is my money, my house, my car, my career, my family, my body"?

Hmmm. God seems to think all of those things belong to Him. You two might want to have a little chat and get on the same page. Not only are there immeasurable benefits that come with that in this life, but I can also tell you, it would be better to do it now before the refining fire.

God's Stuff

In 1 Chronicles 15, King David brings the ark of the covenant back to Jerusalem. It had been stolen by the Philistines, and God cursed them for stealing it, so in desperation, they told the Israelites to take back the ark. It sat in the house of Abinidab for twenty years until David came to claim it. He created a joyous processional celebration for bringing the ark back home to Jerusalem. On the way, a man named Uzza reached out to steady the ark as it was about to slide off the cart. He put his hand on the ark, and *ZAP*, he fell over dead. God sent a clear message: "Don't put your hands on my stuff."

Do you know that your life is God's stuff? All your relationships, all your talents, your body, everything you own, your money, your time, your car, it all belongs to God, and He doesn't want you putting your hands on His stuff or holding them too tightly and trying to keep Him from using them for His glory. So when you stand before the Lord, Jesus will test you with fire to look for His fingerprints on your life. He wants to see the times you prayed, "Not my will but Yours, Lord"; the times you lived out "I am crucified with Christ, yet not I, but Christ in me"; and the times you surrendered your own concerns for His. This is the essence of a true believer, a true bearer of God's image.

How much evidence of God's work is in your life? How much of your life is evidence of His doing? Too many of *your* fingerprints will smother your life and blur your reflected image of God.

Faith Rewards

The house in New York where I grew up was a lot different from the house I live in now. For one, the house I grew up in was fifty-or-so years old and had a lot of things wrong with it. It was a little broken-down but definitely home. The house I live in in California is newer and more modern. I'm sure there are plenty of people who'd view my childhood home as somewhat ghetto, but my years in that house couldn't have been better.

You might think that everyone should have the *same* experience in heaven, but keep in mind that God is creative enough to give everyone an individual, over-the-top, off-the-hook experience that'll ensure that each of us will be incredibly happy and right at home when we get there. If the amount of rewards or crowns that you get in heaven is determined by the amount of faithful deeds that survive the testing fire, it makes sense that we'll all have varied degrees of crowns and rewards. Rewards determine our experience in heaven. If you live by faith and order your life according to the Word of God, you're going to hear, "Well done, good and faithful servant."

First Corinthians 3:11–15 says that if God has been the builder of our life's work, it will endure the fire, and we will be rewarded. If our work has not been done in faith, the work can't tolerate the fire, and we'll suffer loss, although we'll be saved. Laying your rewards at Jesus's feet is one way to worship Him.

> Every time you have an opportunity to take a step of faith, take it. Reward!
> If the Holy Spirit impresses you to pray for somebody, by faith, do it. Reward!
> If the Holy Spirit impresses you to read your Bible, by faith, do it. Reward!

If the Holy Spirit leads you to encourage someone, to give something, to serve somewhere, to sacrifice something, and by faith, you obey—reward, reward, reward!

Airport Drama

It was early in the morning, and I stood in a line for the security check at the airport that practically went the length of New Jersey, and I didn't have much time to catch my flight.

Just as I *finally* got to the front of the line and bent to take my shoes off, a guy in a suit and tie cut directly in front of me. I'd been standing in line forever, the people behind me had been standing in line forever, and this guy cut in front of us instead of going to the end like the rest of us had to.

I wondered if there was a loophole in the Bible that would allow me to jam him up. But you know what I did? I asked God to place His hand on me and direct my thoughts, feelings, and actions. God told me to just *let it go*. Trust me, I'm not saying we should let people walk on us, but it's critical to know that *God calls the shots*. His ways are not our ways, and we need to, by faith, obey Him, especially when it's not our preferred course of action.

Obedience Habit

Shortly after I stopped doing cocaine, I went to a nightclub where I bumped into one of my NFL teammates. Even though the two of us didn't usually get along, he offered me cocaine. Since I had just committed to quit getting high, I said no. I was surprised by how good it felt to say no. I walked away from him, but a few minutes later he offered me cocaine again. Again I said no, and it felt even better.

It was a moment of victory in my life. It was an act of faith that I now know granted a reward in heaven for me, a reward that better equips me to praise my Lord when I get there. I'm also rewarded in this life here and now because I have more freedom to say no to temptation. I never used cocaine ever again.

More Rewards?

You have many opportunities to rack up eternal rewards, but sometimes you rack up some losses because of bad choices. Now before I tell you what needs to happen to turn the losses into gains, let me say this: His hand of discipline sometimes reveals missed opportunities and blessings never realized. You have many opportunities to be a reflection of God's image for His glory. Take a person who surrendered his or her life to the Lord in the last years of their life and a person who lived for Christ since they were a kid, and you'll have two different experiences of heaven. The person who loved and followed Jesus for many years had more experiences with Him and more opportunities to honor Him.

God doesn't compare you with your friends, your parents, or with Mother Teresa. He sees you for you and how well you reflect His image, and He will only hold you accountable for the life He created you to live. My prayer is that you'll allow Jesus to fill your heart like a hand in a glove so you can live the rest of your restored life to its fullest potential.

20

Eternal Glory

Perfected Mirror

Kids from the church often give me pictures they've drawn with their crayons, pencils, and pens. Sometimes I have no idea what these pictures are, but I love getting them anyway. I find myself saying, "Oh how nice!" with a frozen smile on my face. I look at the mom and say under my breath, "What is it?" Then the little kid says, "That's *you* on your bike and that's *me* on my bike, and we are riding to go have a picnic with Jesus and Moses in OZ!" (Hmmm.)

"Oh wow, that'll be fun!" I say.

One little girl named Madison has given me about ten pictures of us together. She started giving them to me when she was about five years old. Every few months she'd give me a new picture she'd made. The pictures had birds, boats, trees, and churches. Sometimes the picture showed the two of us holding hands. Sometimes I'd be preaching and she'd be praying for me. Other times she'd be riding a bike and I'd be up in a tree with my podium reading my Bible. Sometimes she'd color me brown and other times she'd make me yellow or black, depending on which colors of crayons she had that day. Sometimes my hair looked like Buckwheat. Whenever I got these pictures, I'd study all the details and wonder what she was thinking when she drew them.

If God drew a picture of you based on what He's thinking about you, what would it look like? What little details would be included in the picture?

Think about the end of your life. What will your transformation process produce? What will it be like when you, along with your church family, join God in eternity?

Romans 8:18 says that the troubles of this present time aren't worthy to be compared with the glory that one day will be revealed in us. Heaven will be greater than anything you and I can dream about, and my prayer is that you press on and passionately pursue the eternity that God has waiting for you.

God has something very special for His church, and it is worth looking forward to: *a completely perfected reflection of His image*. The only reflection of God's image allowed in heaven is one that perfectly reflects all five aspects of our God image back to Him in a way that's worthy of heaven itself.

Perfect Individuality

During the first day of my first year as a Pop Warner football coach, I noticed a ten-year-old kid standing all alone not knowing where to go. I walked over to help him, even though I wasn't sure where to go either. The process was new to both of us, and feeling lost in a sea of people you don't know can be unnerving. I felt his pain.

You may be someone who could walk through your own church right now and not be noticed because you don't know that many people. But not so in heaven! There, no one will be unknown or go unnoticed! Even in a huge crowd, you will never go unrecognized. We'll always be appreciated, respected, and loved.

Revelation 7:9–10 tells us that there'll be multitudes in heaven praising God all at once:

> After these things I looked, and behold, a great multitude which no one could number, of all nations, tribes, peoples, and tongues, standing before the throne and before the Lamb, clothed with white robes, with palm branches in their hands, and crying out with a loud voice, saying, "Salvation belongs to our God who sits on the throne, and to the Lamb!"

Not only will we each be distinguishable, each of us will have a very personal and individual *experience* with the Lord. Each of us will individually be given our own unique and new name. Revelation 2:17 says, "To the one who conquers I will give some of the hidden manna, and I will give him a white stone, with a new name written on the stone that no one knows except the one who receives it" (ESV).

Your entrance into heaven will be based on your name written in the Lamb's Book of Life (Rev. 21:27). Even though there'll be countless multitudes of souls, you'll always be respected as an *individual* to God. Somehow you'll be part of a crowd, but at the very same time you'll have an *individual* connection with our glorious God who sits on the throne.

God knows us as a church, but more important, He knows us as individuals. It's this individual connection with Him, plus the individual name He gives each of us, that reflect His image. If you have ever felt like you are alone and God has forgotten you, your experience in heaven will be the complete opposite.

Perfected Moral Mirror

Have you ever tapped a crystal glass with a fork to hear its ring? The continued ringing of the glass is the result of the atoms vibrating at the natural frequency of the glass particles. If you touch the glass lightly, the vibration will tickle your finger. If the glass violently vibrated at that frequency for a long time, it would shatter. Singers break glass by singing a note at a frequency that causes the glass to vibrate so violently that it shatters.

Worship is a spontaneous response of respect at the revelation of God. When we're on earth, our worship is partial. Oh yeah, you may be singing with your hands raised and your eyes closed, but from time to time your mind drifts. When you get to heaven, though, every cell and square inch of you will worship in perfect harmony, like glass getting ready to shatter. Your entire being will perfectly and spontaneously reflect and respond to the holiness of God. In heaven we will, with every cell in our being, become completed moral mirrors declaring the moral perfection of God by forever singing out, "Holy, holy, holy is the Lord God Almighty!" (Rev. 4:8 ESV).

First Peter 2:9 declares that we're a *holy* nation of people, a royal priesthood. In heaven we'll experience holiness to a degree that'll bring ecstasy throughout our entire being. The euphoric feeling and excitement of our spiritual body vibrating in perfect worship, along with the countless saints and angels, will be like glass that vibrates to the point of shattering but never breaks, and it will be like this for all eternity as we worship the King of Kings. God will see the glorified unity of all-consuming praise, which is the full impact of His glory reflecting back to Himself.

Eternal Authority

When I was a nineteen-year-old engineering student, I landed a summer job with an engineering firm in New York City. My assignment for the summer was to be an inspector at a construction job in Brooklyn. What did I know about inspecting? Absolutely nothing! But no one else on the job knew that except my supervisor.

One day I decided to test my authority. As they were lowering a slab of concrete into a hole in the middle of the street the size of my living room, I raised my hand and asked to look underneath the slab. Everything halted. Workers started yelling, the crane stopped, and the giant slab of concrete swung back and forth five feet over the hole in the street waiting for the inspector (me) to look under it. I walked under the slab, praying they wouldn't let that thing fall on me, then waved my hand, and they proceeded to lower the slab into the ground. I had no idea what I was doing.

Paul tells us that one day we'll all have positions of authority that today would be way over our heads. First Corinthians 6:2–3 says, "Do you not know that the saints will judge the world? And if the world is to be judged by you, are you unworthy to judge the smallest matters? Do you not know that we shall judge angels? How much more, things that pertain to this life?"

Revelation 20:6 says that we're "blessed and holy" and "shall be priests of God and of Christ" and "shall reign with Him a thousand years." Imagine what it will be like to actually assist the Lord, the King of Kings, in managing His affairs!

Perfect Friendship with God

After a husband and wife take their wedding vows, the husband lifts the veil from the bride's face for the kiss. Often they'll spend a few seconds staring into each other's eyes, and in that intimate moment one might wipe away a tear of the other, or affectionately stroke a cheek.

It's in that moment the two become one, and according to their vows, until death do they part. We'll have a similar intimate moment with God, the lover of our souls. When we enter heaven for an *eternal* relationship with God, we'll also have a very close, intimate relationship with Him.

> And I heard a loud voice from the throne saying, "Behold, the dwelling place of God is with man. He will dwell with them, and they will be his people, and God himself will be with them as their God. He will wipe away every tear from their eyes, and death shall be no more, neither shall there be mourning, nor crying, nor pain anymore, for the former things have passed away." (Rev. 21:3–4 ESV)

There are only a few people we trust to get close enough to wipe away our tears, but this passage takes this idea much further. It shows God's intent to once and for all remove our pain. He'll remove the *stain* of our tears, the *remembrance* of our tears, and even the *possibility* of more tears. All stress, pain, and sorrow will be gone forever, not only because we'll be *with* Him, but also because we'll be *like* Him.

God designed us to enjoy maximum intimacy with Him so we'd be *more than close* to Him. In His image, we're transformed to be *just like Him*. When you see Him face-to-face, you'll be like Him!

> Beloved, we are God's children now, and what we will be has not yet appeared; but we know that when he appears we

shall be like him, because we shall see him as he is. (1 John 3:2–3 ESV)

Eternity brings with it not only the reality of being with God forever but also the reality of being like God. He will not only see Himself in us, but we will also see ourselves in Him. This fulfills the promise He made in Exodus 6:7: "I will take you as My people, and I will be your God. Then you shall know that I am the LORD." We'll finally see Him for who He truly is and we'll truly be one with Him. We'll be able to exclaim, "I once saw dimly, but now I see clearly. I once heard partially, but now I hear Him perfectly." As 1 Corinthians 13:12 says, "Now we see in a mirror dimly, but then face to face. Now I know in part; then I shall know fully, even as I have been fully known" (ESV).

> He will not only see Himself in us, but we will also see ourselves in Him.

The best news of all: this intimate oneness with our God will never end.

Eternal Focus

God's love *never* fails. We have to understand and cling to the powerful truth of the following verses:

Deuteronomy 7:9: Therefore know that the LORD your *God*, He [is] *God*, the faithful *God* who keeps covenant and mercy for a thousand generations with those who *love* Him and keep His commandments.

Romans 5:5: Therefore know that the LORD your *God*, He [is] *God*, the faithful *God* who keeps covenant and mercy for a thousand generations with those who *love* Him and keep His commandments.

Romans 8:38–39: Now hope does not disappoint, because the love of God has been poured out in our hearts by the Holy Spirit who was given to us.

The experience of God's love brings us unmatchable joy today, and in eternity it'll be even greater. His love is endless! There won't be any death in heaven to separate us. It is forever! Our heavenly, over-the-top experience will never end or get old; it will never be less than glorious, and this is where we need to *keep* our focus and hope.

Learning how to ride and handle a motorcycle takes practice, and one of the first things I had to learn was how to turn a corner. The rule is, don't look at the ground in front of you but keep your eye on the end of the curve. If you look down, you go down. Basically, you end up going *where you focus your eyes*.

God created us as eternal beings from an eternal perspective, and His purposes are eternal. You might think the prayers you pray now are just for today, but each prayer should have an eternal component when your eyes are fixed ahead of you, focused on the Lord's purposes.

Paul says in Philippians 3:13–14 that he forgets what's behind and reaches forward to those things that are ahead. He boldly proclaims, "I press toward the goal for the prize of the upward call of God in Christ Jesus." This life is but a blink, but eternity will never end.

Biblical Groaning

We're told in God's Word that not only do we groan as we eagerly wait for the glory of redemption and the manifestation of all that is yet to be revealed, but the earth groans with us. "For we know that the whole creation groans and labors with birth pangs together until now" (Rom. 8:22).

For we know that if our earthly house, this tent, is destroyed, we have a building from God, a house not made with hands, eternal in the heavens. For in this we groan, earnestly desiring to be clothed with our habitation which is from heaven, if indeed, having been clothed, we shall not be found naked. For we who are in this tent groan, being burdened, not because we want to be unclothed, but further clothed, that mortality may be swallowed up by life. Now He who has prepared us for this very thing is God, who also has given us the Spirit as a guarantee. (2 Cor. 5:1–5)

These verses demonstrate that the best of earthly pleasures are only mere shadows of the glory that waits for us in God's presence. So "set your mind on things above and not on things on the earth" (Col. 3:2).

We can get hung up on our cares and concerns instead of aiming toward the "high calling," the "goal." We're doing curves in the road with our eyes focused down on the ground. It's easy to get into the rut of thinking that this life is all there is, and when we take that perspective, we can't see the end of the curve. *Fix your eyes on the eternal prize that God has set before you.*

Your heavenly Father lovingly believes in you, faithfully encourages you, and consistently calls you. Every day, all day, He's looking into the mirror of your life, waiting, watching, and anticipating the day He'll see all of Himself in you. Take a look at yourself in a mirror and tell yourself what God believes for you. The best is yet to come.

What Now?

If you would like to live the life that I have been describing, every aspect of your God image must be completely surrendered to God.

God made you in His image so He can live in and through you but only at your invitation—an invitation that is as simple as ABC: Admit, Believe, Confess.

Admit that you are a sinner. Romans 3:23 says that "all have sinned and fall short of the glory of God."

Tell God that you **Believe** that Jesus is Lord, that He died for your sins and rose from the dead on the third day (Romans 10:9–10). Good Friday and Easter celebrate the weekend that Jesus both died and rose from the dead.

Confess Him as your Savior by asking Him to forgive you and take over your life (1 John 1:9).

If you would like to surrender your life to God, inviting Christ to live inside of your heart and fill every aspect of your God image like a hand does a glove, pray this prayer:

Dear God, I admit that I am a sinner worthy of the punishment my sins deserve. I believe that Jesus is Lord, that He died for my sins and rose from the dead. Jesus, please forgive my sins and come live in my heart. Lord, please transform my character into one that mirrors Your character. Renew my mind to mirror Your mind and change my heart to mirror Your heart.

Thank You, Jesus.

If you prayed that prayer, congratulations. Jesus has just begun a spiritual process of transforming you into His image. For information on your next step, contact me at www.miles mcpherson.com/mirror.

Miles McPherson is the senior pastor of the Rock Church in San Diego and is author of *Do Something: Make Your Life Count*. A former defensive back with the San Diego Chargers, Miles and his wife, Debbie, have three children and live in San Diego.

Visit Miles's website at
www.milesmcpherson.com.

Experience

GOD IN THE MIRROR

with Your Church or Small Group!

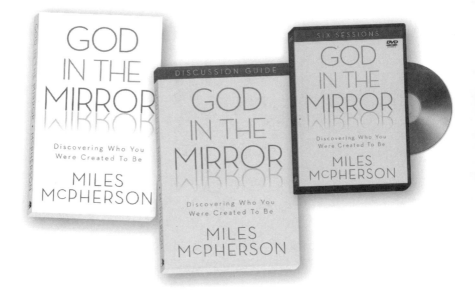

Imagine the power for transformation when everyone in your church is reading, studying, and living the truth that Miles shares in *God in the Mirror*. Everything your church needs to launch and sustain a church-wide preaching and group study experience is provided quickly and simply in one place:

- *Free sermon outlines and resources*
- *Free marketing and promotional materials*
- *Free bonus video and leader training*
- *And more!*

WWW.GODINTHEMIRROR.US